shopping

"Michelle Gonzalez's *Shopping* fashions a delightful tapestry illuminating the borderlands between temptation and tradition, wants and needs. Her incarnational theology refuses an easy Puritanical anti-materialism and suggests a practical reverence for life that can help readers keep shopping—for all its quotidian joys—in its proper place."

Jon Pahl
Professor of History of Christianity
in North America, Gettysburg Seminary
Author of *Shopping Malls and Other Sacred Spaces:
Putting God in Place*

compass

Christian Explorations of Daily Living

David H. Jensen, Series Editor

Playing
James H. Evans Jr.

Shopping
Michelle A. Gonzalez

Forthcoming Volumes

Working
Darby Kathleen Ray

Eating and Drinking
Elizabeth Groppe

Parenting
David H. Jensen

shopping

Michelle A. Gonzalez

Fortress Press
Minneapolis

SHOPPING
Compass series
Christian Explorations of Daily Living

Cover design: Laurie Ingram
Book design: Christy J. P. Barker

Library of Congress Cataloging-in-Publication Data

Gonzalez, Michelle A.
 Shopping : Michelle A. Gonzalez.
    p. cm. — (Compass)
 Includes bibliographical references.
   ISBN 978-0-8006-9727-3 (pbk. : alk. paper) 1. Consumption (Economics)—Religious aspects--Christianity. 2. Consumption (Economics)—Moral and ethical aspects—United States. I. Title.
 BR115.C67G66 2010
 241'.68—dc22
                                    2010010688

The paper used in this publication meets the minimum requirements of American National Standard for Information Sciences—Permanence of Paper for Printed Library Materials, ANSI Z329.48-1984.

Manufactured in the U.S.A.
14 13 12 11 10   1 2 3 4 5 6 7 8 9 10

contents

foreword

Shopping is integral to everyday life. In order to obtain the basic necessities of life, such as food, clothing, and shelter, most of us shop. Shopping, at this basic level, is especially pertinent in a globalized economy. It connects the shopper to people who harvest crops, stitch clothing, and build houses. Shopping is also connected to other practices that have been central to Christian faith from its earliest days, practices such as gift-giving and hospitality. Many of us shop and buy things so that we might give to others. In twenty-first-century American life, however, shopping displays an added function as an end in itself or as an end that secures other ends, such as economic growth, patriotism, or sheer entertainment. Over the past several years, several political leaders have told us to shop for the common good of our nation. Advertising often suggests that shopping offers pleasures uniquely its own. Shopaholics will attest that for them the process of shopping itself is more important than the goods acquired (or given away) through shopping. For many in our day, we shop not in order to live but live in order to shop.

What does Christian faith say about shopping? Quite a bit, according to Michelle Gonzalez in this engaging and accessible study. By attending closely to Scripture, Catholic social teachings, and the actual experience of shopping in our hyper-connected world, Gonzalez offers a vision of shopping that avoids the extremes of American consumerism (shop until you drop; live to shop) and Christian anti-materialism (all shopping is sinful and the goods acquired through shopping are corrupt). In the process, she turns our attention to the beauty of human handiwork as well as the ugliness of exploitation caused by inhuman forms of shopping. The result is a much-needed reformulation of shopping that more nearly reflects the justice, beauty, and wholeness central to Christian faith.

David H. Jensen

introduction

Outside my office I have a bulletin board full of cartoons. All of them—except one—are from Boondocks, the sharp Aaron McGruder comic strip that looks at political, racial, and social justice issues. The one exception is a Bizarro cartoon that shows a priest sitting in a confessional. From behind the screen an unidentified penitent communicates via cartoon bubble, "I sell shoes for Prada."

This cartoon resonates with me for many reasons, but the most important for our purposes is the shame and guilt this poor soul feels for his job at a high-end Italian designer retail shop. While I would not sit behind the confessional screen and say, "I work at Prada," I would whisper, "I wish I could buy Prada." Why the guilt? The other cartoons may clue you in. I consider myself a Roman Catholic deeply informed by a commitment to social justice, solidarity with the poor, and attentiveness to issues of identity that the Boondocks cartoons, while not religious, represent. And yet I would love to own some Prada, knowing very well that for the cost of one Prada bag a family of ten in my husband's Guatemalan hometown of San Lucas Tolimán could be fed for a year. I feel guilty about wanting the Prada. I know it is wrong, yet I still want it. A Catholic confessional is a perfect venue for such a crisis of faith and values.

This book emerges from that struggle. In this short volume I explore the everyday practice of shopping and its implications for Christians globally. My context and intended audience are American Christians who wrestle with an understanding of their religion and faith life that is critical of the consumerism, capitalism, and gluttonous consumption that characterize dominant American culture. Yet we have to shop, and some of you may confess along with me that we like to shop. We often confuse things that we want with things that we need. In our particular society, we are constantly encouraged to buy. In fact, I suspect only in the United States is shopping seen as a way of fighting terrorism (the mantra post-September 11) and a means of helping our country get out of debt. Whether it is billboards, television, or magazines, we are surrounded by the lure of the car, the dress, and the flat-screen television. Apple's iPhone, perhaps one of the most brilliant products from one of the best promoters of consumerism, not only keeps you wanting to buy a new one with each new version but also has you busy buying applications for the iPhone you already own. It is a product of consumption that seemingly requires more consumerism.

I consider myself a Catholic informed by Jesus' often quoted pronouncement, "No one can serve two masters; for a slave will either hate the one and love the other, or be devoted to the one and despise the other. You cannot serve God and wealth" (Matt 6:24). I read Christian social teaching's defense of the worker and critique of capitalism; I resonate with liberation theology's solidarity with the poor; I meditate on the various instances in Scripture where we are encouraged if not required to put God before material goods. Yet I also live in the twenty-first-century United States. I am a college professor and therefore, in the global economic sphere, an extremely wealthy individual. I constantly struggle with that fine line between want and need, comfort and excess. I am well aware that some of the items I purchase are created or cultivated by workers who do not receive just pay. I am equally aware that even those low-paying jobs are sometimes the only source of income they have.

This book explores the tensions and struggles I have outlined above. Essentially, the book attempts to answer the following questions: Can you be a committed Christian who likes to shop? Is shopping sinful? Can our love of goods impede our relationship with the sacred? As you may have surmised from my earlier comments, this is not going to be an anti-materialist book that condemns all shopping as sinful. However, I also will not fall on the other extreme, condoning the materialism that has come to dominate our country in ways that make people easily value objects over people. Somewhere in the middle, in the tensions of our everyday lives, we will find a clearer sense of how we do and how we should shop.

The book is divided into three chapters. The first gives an overview of American consumerism, debt, and the manner in which materialism has come to mark us as a capitalist society. This "thick description" of the practice of shopping will contextualize our everyday acts of consumerism in light of the global economy. In other words, even the most casual purchase can connect us to men, women, and children across the world. How we in the United States spend our money has a major impact on the global poor.

Various theological issues will be raised in this chapter. Fundamental is the broader question of the materialism that saturates American society. What is the Christian response to the ease with which we value objects over people? The carefree manner in which American Christians purchase, for example, clothing and coffee, knowing well that said items are often produced by exploited workers, is baffling. The very existence of fair trade coffee and sweatshop-free clothing should force us to confront the fact that those items that do not bear these seals are often produced in dehumanizing conditions. In the United States, the overconsumption of goods and material accumulation has become the norm and not the exception. This excess is a hallmark of American culture and society.

Another issue is globalization. Through our shopping we become concretely connected to those individuals across the globe who cultivate and produce the goods we purchase. This is a tricky reality to navigate, for what may seem to us in the United States as unjust labor practices can sometimes be the only employment for millions across the globe. Which is worse, a job that exploits or no job at all? In the United States we are often detached from the production of the goods we consume. This became clear to me during the two years I lived in a coffee region in Guatemala. Seeing the intense process of cultivating, picking, carrying, cleaning, and processing coffee, as well as how little farm workers are paid for this work, has made me never sip a cup of coffee in the same way. This book encourages the reader to think more concretely about the processes and people that are involved in the goods we purchase and consume. In this section we also discuss religious consumerism. I focus on the ways in which religious objects and rituals have become consumerist products. In addition, we enter into the intersection of religious dress and fashion, examining how clothing is not only a symbol of religious identity but also a product of consumerism.

The book's second chapter will examine Christian approaches to shopping. Here I tap into sources that can inform a Christian response to the issues outlined in the previous section. I draw primarily from two dimensions of the Christian tradition: Scripture and Roman Catholic social teaching. The goal of this chapter is to give the reader a Christian framework to address the global context in which we shop. The Scripture section examines various key biblical passages that shed light on consumerism, materialism, and the practice of shopping. My examination of Catholic social teaching is an attempt to demonstrate how one Christian denomination has explicitly addressed some of the critical, global issues raised previously. This chapter, much like the previous one, is merely a snapshot to invite the reader into a more comprehensive examination of his or her faith tradition and spirituality. My focus on Catholic social teaching is based on its legacy of demonstrating the institutional church's concern for the marginalized in capitalist societies. It is a clear example of Christianity's attention to the poor in light of the common good. Catholic social teachings, however, often emphasize the structural at the expense of the everyday. This section will connect its broad, structural theological critique to everyday life.

In the final chapter I propose a constructive reconfiguration of the practice of shopping. How can we understand shopping in light of the Christian responses explored in the previous section? What does it mean to be a Christian consumer in this globalized world? What are the implications for Christian theology and spirituality if we take seriously the everyday practice of shopping? This project hopes to highlight more concretely our daily lives and practices and the manner in which our faith is and should be integrated more explicitly into the everyday decisions that we make, often without thinking of their broader, global impact.

Far from presenting spirituality as a compartmentalized dimension of our lives, *Shopping* places the Christian faith concretely at the center of what many would argue is a frivolous act. But in this final chapter, I also bring the importance of embodiment and aesthetics into the mix. Too often, an attention to the body and one's appearance is seen as a hindrance to one's relationship with the sacred. This text will argue quite the opposite, presenting a celebration of one's appearance as part of one's faith life. However, given the themes of social justice highlighted throughout the text, there is a fine line between the celebration of one's appearance and superficial materialism.

The goal of the project is to examine how everyday life is shaped by Christian faith. Contrary to an understanding of spirituality that sees spirituality in isolation from one's life and occurs in explicitly religious settings, an emphasis on everyday practices demonstrates the manner in which our spirituality saturates our lives. *Shopping* will examine how consumerism, materialism, and globalization intersect in the act of purchasing goods. Ultimately, this book attempts to address how we as Christians should understand our relationship to shopping in light of the Christian message.

Daily life is the foundation of the societal webs that shape our world. This book will be attentive to the interrelationship between the everyday and the structural. The very act of buying a piece of clothing, for example, in a large retailer in the United States, in this globalized economy, can link you to a poor factory worker in the global South. As Christians, how do we respond to that connection? How do Christian justice and solidarity affect how we value and spend our money? Exploring these and other questions will be the focus of this book. Underlying the text is the thesis that how much we shop, the way we shop, and what we shop for has a direct impact on our faith lives.

1

shopping

american consumerism and globalization

I stand with one of my students on the shores of Lake Atitlan, one of the most beautiful places in Guatemala, if not the world. I have brought a group of undergrads to San Lucas Tolimán, my husband's hometown on the lake, to work with the Roman Catholic mission's social justice outreach with the local Mayan community. My student is bartering with what looks like a nine-year-old boy. He is selling necklaces and earrings and charging $4 a necklace. The young woman does not want to pay "that much." She talks the boy down to two necklaces and two sets of earrings for $4. Throwing her jewelry in a backpack overflowing with her other purchases, textiles and purses in colorful Mayan patterns, she triumphantly looks at me and says, "Did you see that? I am getting so good at this." I look at her, then I look at the boy, whose mother has called him over and is scolding him for selling too much for too little. I want to cry or throw up or both.

This student is a good kid. She has an awareness of social justice. She has enthusiastically moved rocks and plants and done all of the volunteer labor that a trip to San Lucas entails. She is passionate about service. In fact, all of the students on this trip are good kids. They are the type of students that I find comfort in, knowing that one day they will be leaders. They don't drink a lot and are studious and really care about issues of global poverty. And yet with a mixture of horror and nausea, I have watched most of these bright, committed students haggle with poor Mayans over a dollar or two. After such bargaining they usually comment that since they only saved a dollar or two it is really no big deal, and they begin to view their bargaining as a challenge, a sport, a contest. Knowing that the average family in San Lucas has at least ten children and subsists on maybe $120 per month, I know full well that a dollar or two is a huge deal to these sellers. Yet I am silent.

I have taken various groups to San Lucas and lived there for two years. I have watched the same thing happen over and over again when it comes to shopping. Visitors of all ages are thrilled to find beautiful things for so cheap, yet they want them to be even cheaper. I watch as beautiful textiles are bartered over, textiles that for many are the ultimate symbol of Mayan pride and culture. For Mayans, maintaining traditional dress, or *traje* as it is called, is a reflection of pride in one's heritage. This slowly dying practice is being replaced by Western dress, and many scholars see the demise of this outward symbol of Mayan culture as an indicator of the assimilation of Mayan culture as a whole. Visitors and tourists from the United States get caught up in the thrill

> The gap in our economy is between what we have and what we think we ought to have—and that is a moral problem, not an economic one.
>
> *Paul Heyne*

of the cheap purchase made even cheaper by their skillful bargaining.

I do not know why I keep silent. Do I barter, you may ask? I don't ever. My husband does, though for him it is because he, as a native, wants the "Guatemalan" price and not the tourist price. I do not speak out because I am conflicted. I know prices are raised for tourists, again only a dollar or two, so in many ways most tourists who bargain get the standard price. I also know that it is better to make a sale than no sale at all. I think what bothers me about these transactions is the thrill I see in people's eyes as they find a cheap deal. That even in the midst of this Mayan town, where there is illiteracy and contaminated water, in the midst of individuals spending their hard-earned money to travel to volunteer in this impoverished community, American consumerism still prevails.

I Shop, therefore I Am

It would not be an exaggeration to state that the American economy is based on consumption. This country describes shopping as a form of psychological counseling, otherwise known as retail therapy. We rack up thousands in credit card debt. And many of us refuse to accept the fact that living within our means is not satisfactory, desirable, or to put it bluntly, enough. It would seem that we always want more no matter what we have, and the consumer appetite is insatiable.

The United States is not the only country shaped by consumerism. However, the insatiability of American consumerism is one of its hallmarks. Consumerism in our country is based on the creation of new things for us to desire and want and a constant need for the new. In other words, an element of our consumerist culture is to keep us dissatisfied, always wanting more and never content with what we have. There is a lack of temperance in contemporary American culture's capitalist economy. The value of sufficiency is entirely distorted and excess is normative. We find it difficult to distinguish between what we want and what we need, and we are constantly barraged with images and advertisements that attempt to convince us of the inadequacies in our lives that can be solved with one outfit, one electronic gadget. Material goods are presented as the solution to all of our problems, yet the consumer is constantly presented with new material goods in a constant cycle of the thrill of the purchase, the enjoyment of the object, a growing sense of dissatisfaction or boredom, followed by a renewed zeal as a new consumer good appears on the horizon.

All of us shop. Shopping unites humanity, though we all shop in varying degrees. When I lived in a Mayan community in Guatemala, I would shop three times a week at the *mercado* (local street market). Granted, my shopping was limited primarily to fruits, vegetables, and other foods, but it was shopping nonetheless. Those market days were the most vibrant and energetic days in town. The community was abuzz with the possibility of something new, something different, entering into their lives.

Here in the United States, we have created a culture where we need to cultivate the art of shopping. We used to need to know how to sew; now we need to know how to shop. A small percentage of our population makes its own clothes. We are dependent on the sewing of others, often in questionable conditions, a point I will turn to later in this chapter. On top of the need to know how to shop for pure necessity's sake, our economy is dependent on it. If we went into stores only when we needed something, the economy would collapse. Our economy is entirely dependent on our excessive consumerism. The retail market is oversaturated. There are too many stores, too many goods, and too many options. And while we can discuss the limitation of consumption in order to avoid hedonism and the virtue of frugality, that limitation would greatly affect this country's economy.

> Wealth consists not in having great possessions but in having few wants.
> *Esther De Waal*

You may be saying that this may be the case for the majority of individuals living in the United States, but that this is not you. You find value in different, more meaningful things: family, friendships, religion, and work. You are "in" a consumerist culture but not "of" that culture. However, we accept cultural values whether we admit it or not. Unless we are actively seeking to undermine consumerism, we are part of consumerist culture. Our consumerism also reflects our societal values as a whole. How we consume, what we consume, and how those goods are produced reflects a culture's values. A country that turns a blind eye to unjust labor practices in order to have cheaper material goods is a country that values the price of a product over the life of the worker. Similarly, a country that consumes excessively, knowing that the percentage of what we consume as a population grossly outweighs the percentage of our population globally, is a country that cares little about depleting the world's resources.

Consumerism is an ideology. It promotes a value system that is staunchly against the core of Christian values. Consumerism values having and enjoying over serving, loving, and giving. Consumerism centers on ownership, on pleasure. When I see the word consumerism, the root "consume" jumps out at me. To consume is to devour. I liken it to eating. And no matter how much we eat, we always, inevitably, will get hungry again. And such is the case with material goods. Once we unleash our appetite for objects, we fall into a helpless cycle of consumption, satisfaction, and hunger.

Yet while consumerism is against the core of Christian values, this does not mean it does not have its own spirituality. Consumerism is not the rejection of spirituality for materialism; consumerism can be a type of spirituality. One's identity, one's worldview, comes to be shaped by the goods that they own. Shopping becomes leisure time, family time, a way to bond with friends. In order to mourn after September 11, we are told to shop. Shopping provides a sense of comfort and stability. When people stop shopping it evokes a sense of insecurity in our future. We begin to worry about jobs, the economy, and our future. This is understandable. As stated above, our economy is based on our rabid consumption of goods.

Consumerism is romantic and exciting. Consumerism represents a certain restlessness with things; what you buy is never enough and the object never totally satisfies. You are always left wanting more, and inevitably, the market will provide you with more. Whether it is a new car with revolutionary features, a new phone that makes your one-month-old phone seem helplessly outdated, or the article of clothing you love that has become miraculously out of fashion overnight, the market and our culture sets the stage for these feelings of inadequacy. Even academics, whether they admit to it or not, are part of this consumer culture. Whether it is the business of higher education or the business of selling books, our livelihood depends in part on this consumerist economy.

Disposable Goods, Disposable People

I remember the first time I walked into a Starbucks. I was in college at Georgetown, and a friend took me to some "Seattle coffee place" in Dupont Circle. It was a fifteen-minute drive to get there, and when we arrived I was greeted by people sitting around reading and drinking coffee. This did not surprise me per se. I had just returned from my junior year abroad in Paris, so individuals lingering over coffee cups were not a strange sight for me. Yet it was odd in the United States. And while I can remember my first time in Starbucks, I cannot for the life of me remember much about life before Starbucks. The same is true for major bookstores such as Barnes & Noble and Borders. As a child I vaguely remember walking into a bookstore, selecting a book, and paying for it. Now I walk into a major chain, get a coffee, read magazines, and watch my kids read books and play with toys provided for them. My two-year-old can say Starbucks. I am a product and a promoter of this consumerism.

I know that once upon a time there were more independent bookstores and coffee shops, and that coffee and whipped cream did not necessarily seem like obvious partners. The growth of chains such as Starbucks and Barnes & Noble represents one of the most dreaded effects of consumerism, the homogenization of society. So now everywhere in the United States you see the same storefronts and consume the same product. Gone, and excuse the pun, is the local flavor of places. This is sometimes described as globalization when one examines this economic and cultural homogenization from a global perspective. In addition to homogenization, the impact of these chains is that they introduce into the market new items that suddenly seem essential to us. Coffee comes to resemble milkshakes and the size of our hot beverages look more like small buckets than drinks. I suspect this super-sizing and sugar-izing also contributes to the growing obesity of our nation, yet another sign that gluttony of food and of goods has become normative in the United States.

Our appetite for material goods is based on the notion that these goods have value. Yet that value is imposed by the market place. A designer t-shirt priced at $300 and a Target t-shirt priced at $15 are really not that radically different. The fashion industry is entirely based on the idea that a designer label, or a name, costs more. Yet the value of that designer is entirely a construction. To be fair, there is handmade clothing, exclusive fabrics and leathers, and workmanship that would require more labor to be put into a garment, consequently raising its price. But ultimately, clothing is there to cover our nakedness and protect us from the elements. The value of fashion is entirely constructed. On the other side of the spectrum are the extremely cheap clothing items, what I like to call disposable clothing. Stores like Forever 21, H&M, and Charlotte Russe sell "affordable" clothing that individuals purchase and wear one or two times because it is (1) too trendy to wear more than that; and (2) because its quality is so poor it often begins to fall apart after a few wears. These are disposable in terms of style and quality.

> We used to build civilizations. Now we build shopping malls.
> *Bill Bryson*

The fashion industry is at the center of us seeing, ultimately, all clothing as obsolete way before its time. Fashion retires clothing long before its usability (to cover and protect us) has expired. Fashion, ultimately, is fake. Yet the transient nature of goods is not exclusive to the fashion world. Electronics rise and fall based on their innovative technology that is rendered obsolete within days of the product's release. Similarly, the food industry is constantly introducing the new miracle foods that can save your life. I am not arguing against technological innovation or scientific discoveries about the benefits of the food we eat. However, this is also a moneymaking industry based on our desire to buy and continue to buy to keep ahead with the market.

Because material goods are transient and disposable, they have little authentic value for us. Material objects give us a false sense of security; at the same time, they are transient, have little history, and do not have much meaning for us. I do not care very much about the iPod, the blouse, or the gaming system, because I know they will not be in my life very long. But I do care about the photos, clothing, and other little gadgets my mother has saved for me and my children throughout her life. They represent her (my) history and her (my) identity. I cannot say the same about many of the material objects in my life, and I often wonder what mementos I will pass on to my children: an old Blackberry? Gap jeans? our Wii? The goods that clutter our homes do not have inter-personal value in the way family mementos do.

In addition to having little personal value, much of what we consume is an abstraction. In other words, we have no connection to who makes it or where it comes from. We have little awareness of the labor that goes into the everyday things in our lives. This hit home hard for me after living in Guatemala. My husband's hometown is in a coffee region. I would watch as Mayan farmers cultivated the coffee for months. Then in November, I would see them descend down the mountains with one hundred pound bags of coffee on their backs. The coffee was then weighed and farmers were paid. Those in charge of the production would remove the beans from the coffee fruit, process it, and then lay it out on concrete terraces to dry for several days. The coffee was then sorted by hand to remove any bad beans and finally toasted, ground, and packaged. Months of labor for our morning cup of joe.

I have never been able to drink coffee in the same way after living there, and I can only stare blankly around my home and wonder about the many faceless hands, the months that go into the things that surround me. When we purchase goods in stores we are far removed from those who produce them. Shopping *en el mercado* is a personal interaction unlike consumer shopping. There I would come face to face with farmers, the actual individuals that have grown the food I was going to consume. While farmers' markets are becoming increasingly popular today, we have a long way to go regarding our connection with those who produce what we purchase.

Shopping as Entertainment and Lifestyle

We cannot discuss consumerism without addressing what I like to describe as the evangelization of advertising. As I mentioned earlier, we are constantly bombarded with images that tell us what to buy and what should be desirable to us. Advertising is everywhere. Awards shows like the Oscars, Golden Globes, and Grammys are virtual fashion shows where actors and artists are asked what they are wearing long before the film or performance they are being recognized for is mentioned. It is how they look, and not what they have done, that becomes the center of attention.

Consumerism has even seeped into the television programs we watch. Consumerism is part of entertainment. Shows like *Sex and the City* began a nationwide obsession with Manolo Blahnik shoes (at least for women and some men). Oprah's post-Thanksgiving show on her "favorite things" initiates frenzies over items. One can rest assured that if an item is featured on Oprah's show, it most likely will sell out. Makeover shows integrate consumerism and entertainment. *What Not to Wear*, a popular makeover show on The Learning Channel, offers "poorly" dressed participants $5000 to throw away their wardrobe and purchase a new one. Hair and makeup are included, and male contributors are also featured on the show. Many of these individuals tell painful stories of weight gain, deaths in the family, or just being over-extended in life as the reasons behind their "frumpiness." At the end of the show, a brand new, often teary man or woman stands before us, claiming that their new clothes make them look better and that they now feel better as well. Their lives seem better after shopping and a little hair dye. And for those of us who watch the show (and yes, I confess that I watch it), what do we do for the greater part of an hour? We watch someone shop.

These types of shows are not limited to women. The now-cancelled *Queer Eye for the Straight Guy* took male participants, gave them makeovers, and redid their homes. These makeovers are sold as a new beginning, a turning point in people's lives. Perhaps they are. However, the integration of consumerism with television (and there are a pile of home makeover shows I could also list here) is a devious way to send us the message that if we shop we can change and that change will be for the better.

I realize that shopping can be innocent, yet not all shopping is innocent. There are some very strong downfalls to our emphasis on consumerism that can lead to extremely destructive practices and values. Too often what we own comes to own us. Those things that we should truly value have no monetary value. We become obsessed with material goods. Objects take precedence over relationships, over flesh and blood human beings. Unlike other relationships, with shopping we are defined by our relationship with objects and the values imposed upon them by society.

Modern conveniences are in many ways a mixed blessing: We become dependent on them, and they depersonalize our relationships. I cannot tell you how many times I have emailed a colleague whose office is two doors down from me instead of getting up to have face-to-face interaction. We live in a world where consumer goods become indicators of social status. Here in the United States we no longer compare ourselves to our neighbors, but instead to the wealthy as we try to emulate them. I suspect that tabloid journalism, reality television, and the abundance of blogs and websites that tell us exactly what gadget someone is carrying, what car they are driving, and what clothes they are wearing play a key role in this. Branding becomes a way for us to construct our

> Buying is a profound pleasure.
>
> *Simone de Beauvoir*

identity. Through our clothing we are able to assume new identities.

In addition to "branding our identity," our value becomes reduced to our economic prosperity and we are reduced to our marketability and productivity. Our status is defined by material objects. Success is defined by economic success. I cannot tell you the sadness I feel when I hear the majority of the undergraduates I teach discuss the sole purpose of their education as a means to obtain a good job and make lots of money. Now, I am not naïve. Many students today incur massive debt to receive higher education. However, education has become a means to an end and does not have value in and of itself. Everything becomes a commodity, even ideas. This became very clear with the economic downturn in 2008. Numerous articles claimed the death of the humanities since they were not economically viable fields of study. After all, what value does a poem have in consumerist culture?

Many in the United States live in a vicious cycle of excessive labor in order to be able to spend money. We work harder so we can consume more, which ends up taking away our time from family, friends, and volunteer work. We don't see work as an end in itself but what entitles us to spend. Our work serves our lifestyle but is not in any way pleasurable in and of itself. I often wonder if this obsession with shopping signals a deeper malaise in our society. Do we just settle for what is given to us? In other words, if contemporary society does not give us a sense of meaningful community or value in our work, do we just "settle" for goods? I will probe this deeper in the final chapter of this book. Ultimately, what we buy and how we buy not only reflects how we value others, it is also a reflection of how we value ourselves.

Consuming the Earth, Consuming the Poor

In my introductory comments I stated that in light of the global economy, or to put it more precisely, in light of the global poor, I am in fact rich. Middle-class Americans don't like to think of themselves as rich. This is due, I suspect, to the fact that we define rich as excessive wealth. Rich people do not have to worry about money. Rich people can buy anything that they want. However, if we examine middle-class wealth in the United States in terms of the global population, the middle class is indeed rich. As the United Nations 2007 Human Development Report indicates, the poorest 40 percent of the world's population has 5 percent of the world's wealth (http://hdr.undp.org/en/). Nearly half of the world's children live in poverty.

The wealth of the United States allows us to consume close to 25 percent of the world's energy when we only constitute 5 percent of the global population (http://hdr .undp.org/en/). As the website www.mindfully.org points out, there are more shopping malls in the United States than high schools. The culture of consumption in the United States has environmental implications that affect the globe. The earth does not have an infinite amount of resources, yet here in the United States we exploit those resources as if they are exclusively ours and are endless. The rest of the world could not consume in the way we do here in the States, for all of our resources would run out at an alarming rate. This culture of consumption is fairly new in the history of the United States. Only in the twentieth century did we gain the resources and technology to become the mass consumers that we are today. So while our desire to consume excessively has always been with us, our ability to do so is a recent phenomenon.

In addition to setting us apart from the majority of the world's population, the wealth and consumption that dominates the United States also isolates "us" from "them." Wealth gives us the ability to seclude ourselves from the poor. Too often we call that isolation protection. The classic example of this is the gated community. In addition, our wealth allows us to drive around neighborhoods that are suspect (that is, poor) and avoid poverty if we desire. This is radically different from countries in the global South. While cities in these countries may have exclusive, gated communities, it is very difficult to avoid the massive poverty of the majority of their populations.

These populations in Africa, Latin America, the Caribbean, and parts of Asia became the foundation of the cheap labor force that creates the very goods that we purchase. Many of these workers labor in horrible conditions that have a dramatic impact on their health. Their pay is minimal. We are told to shop until we drop, but it is the workers that drop, often from malnutrition, poor ventilation, or an excessive amount of consecutive hours in a factory or field. More and more American corporations are turning to work forces abroad because the labor is cheaper and seemingly endless. This is perhaps one of the more difficult issues we need to wrestle with. Through our consumerism we participate in global slavery, whether we admit to it or not. Slavery today is much different than the slavery that was characteristic of the transatlantic slave trade. Today slavery is more about control of a workforce than ownership. Unlike the transatlantic slave trade of the past, today we have a seemingly endless supply of faceless, nameless workers that can create the objects of our consumption cheaply. Technology often contributes to the dehumanization of workers. Did not the invention of the cotton gin lead to the escalation of the slave trade to the United States? The invention made the production easier, but cheap labor was still needed to pick the cotton.

Has the consumer replaced the worker as the central concern of our economy? Karl Marx famously argued in the nineteenth century that workers are alienated from what they produce. The fruits of their labor are objectified, and it is the employer and not the worker who owns what is produced. In many ways echoing my argument above, Marx argued that there exists what he named a commodity fetish: Goods are not valuable in and of themselves but consumers place value on them. Value is an abstraction and the object becomes a cultural commodity. An example of this is designer fashion. Yet with all of Marx's concern for the worker, I am not sure workers are so important anymore. It is the consumer and the demands of the consumer economy that dominates. The worker is at the mercy of the consumer.

Interestingly, with all of the emphasis on consumption, how much we own (and shopping itself) can be both a source of guilt and pride. Shopping is something that, thanks to the revolution of the Internet, we can now do in secret. We need to find a balance between living well and living with shame. For some, not only how we shop but even the fact that we shop is suspect. Attention to one's appearance is seen as a form of vanity in certain circles. Last year an article appeared describing college professors as the worst-dressed professionals. There is a sense within the academy that attention to one's appearance is frivolous and detracts from the attention one places on their serious scholarship and teaching. One's intelligence is challenged if one looks too good.

This is especially an issue for women, who are fairly new to the academy as a whole and, for better or worse, are much more engaged with the fashion industry. No matter what the sphere, women overwhelmingly do most of the shopping for the home (that is, groceries). Shopping even today is still "women's work." In terms of women and fashion, there is a strong connection between women's clothing and religious identity. Many fascinating studies exist that look at how proscriptions on women's dress across the world's religions are both a source of oppression and empowerment. Whether it is the Muslim veil, the Catholic habit, or the Indian sari, there are deep connections between women's identity, culture, holiness, and dress. Often modesty is associated with holiness within religious settings. Similarly, a woman who pays a lot of attention to her appearance is automatically stereotyped at best as vain and in a worst-case scenario as unintelligent.

> The corruption of the American soul is consumerism.
>
> *Ben Nicholson*

One point of contention among feminists since the inception of the modern women's movement has been dress and its relationship to gender empowerment. Within religious circles, dress can also indicate one's religious authority for both men and women. Fashion and religion go hand in hand. It is appropriate that we mention the connection between fashion and religion, for now as we turn to religious consumerism, I would like to begin with one of the most consumerist religious rituals, one from my own cultural background: *la quinceañera*.

Shopping Religion

The *quinceañera* stands before me and my oldest son, who is four. His jaw drops when his eyes fall upon her and he whispers in my ear, "Is she a princess?" The question is not surprising. The young woman is in a floor-length strapless pink gown, her hair piled on her head with a tiny tiara, and dozens of women, young and old, are fussing over the dress, the makeup, the girl.

What is a *quinceañera?* It is the name of both a rite of passage and the young woman. In many Latin American countries and consequently also in the United States among Latino/as, there has been a tradition of celebrating a young woman's fifteenth birthday with a ritual and party. The ritual has traditionally been a Roman Catholic mass said in her honor. The party that follows is a celebration for family and friends. However, today the party has eclipsed the mass, and what was once a religious-based rite of passage has become a money-making industry. *Quinceañeras* now have extravagant parties where the religious element is often just a prayer said by a priest before dinner. Families spend thousands of dollars for these festivities, and it has become a major commercial industry. There are *quinceañera* cruises, photo shoots, and so on; the list is endless. The last time I was at Target, there was an entire quinceañera display: cake cutters, candles, dolls, and albums. Girls often have a court of friends for their party, and in a strong sense it has become more like an American "sweet sixteen" than a Latin American ritual.

I did not have a *quinceañera*, yet I have attended many both in the United States and abroad. What shocks me today is that they have been transformed from a ritual and celebration to just a party. No longer is a young Latina's fifteenth year ceremonially celebrated in the context of the traditions and religion of her family. Today *quinceañeras* are huge expensive parties, where in some cases families go into debt in order to pay for them. The commercialization of the *quinceañera* parallels a larger commercialization of religious rituals and objects as a whole, yet another characteristic of American consumer culture. I liken it in many ways to the consumerism that has come to surround the bar mitzvah and bat mitzvah in Jewish circles.

We are forced to ask: Has consumerism undermined tradition? I find it fascinating that part of the commercialization of these rites of passage is that they provide ways in which immigrant groups show they have succeeded. In other words, for an immigrant Latino/a family in the United States, a big quince party is a way of showing their families and their friends that they have achieved success. The party becomes a manner of showcasing the family's economic position.

The commercialization of religious rituals and objects is not new. We only have to look at Christmas in the United States, the use of Buddhist prayer beads and Catholic rosaries as jewelry, or the red kabbalah string as a fashion statement. However, there is a danger in the removal of religious objects and rituals from their belief base, for in that process they lose the very foundation of beliefs that made them significant. Through consumerism, religious beliefs are divorced from symbols and practices.

When the commodification of religion leads to religion as a cultural resource, belief ceases to be an element of practice. In present-day Cuba, for example, there is what I call Santería tourism. For a fee tourists can go on a Santería (an African Diaspora religion) tour that shows them an "authentic" ritual. This ritual is merely a show put on for tourists, yet the outsider is fooled into thinking he or she is witnessing authentic religious practices. Religions, like all elements of human culture, have become products of consumerism, yet in the process religion becomes stripped of its meaning and value.

The commercialization of religion is blatantly found in the relationship between shopping and religious holidays. What marks the Christmas season in the United States? I can tell you one thing: it is not an Advent calendar or lighting a candle on an Advent wreath. Instead it is Black Friday, the biggest shopping day of the year. Situated on the Friday after Thanksgiving, it actually co-opts two holidays at once. Shopping comes to dominate the end of each year, and the eternal search for a bargain becomes the country's mantra. The consumer becomes overwhelmed by the quest for cheap presents.

> Earth provides enough to satisfy every man's need but not every man's greed.
>
> *Mohandas K. Gandhi*

In many ways the Internet makes this even more pronounced, for now you can sit at home and shop. Shopping has become a religion in the United States. The tag line for the 2009 documentary *The September Issue*, which focuses on the creation of Vogue magazine's September issue, is: "Fashion is a religion. This is the Bible." There are websites, blogs, and discussion groups dedicated to the act of shopping. Online communities such as fashion ism.org are discussion boards that center on shopping and fashion but also create a social network of predominantly women to discuss health, beauty, parenting, and home décor. Participants are able to post anonymously yet simultaneously build community across the globe. These websites are valuable for individuals worldwide, as the explosion of them in the past decade indicates. But I often wonder whether these communities have come to replace face-to-face communities (that is, book clubs, volunteer organization, religious groups, and so on).

The United States claims to be a secular state, yet Christianity is the dominant religion and clearly influences the values and rituals of this country. The "God" of "in God we trust" on our money most likely is not Allah. The same can be said of the God we speak of when we pledge we are "one nation under God." The way we structure holidays and leisure time is often framed by the Christian framework. Our presidents often make speeches and cite Scripture. Christian discourse is part of the dominant discourse, and other religious traditions do not come close to its impact and influence. Moral issues such as abortion, same-sex marriage, and stem cell research often become dominated by Christian debate and rhetoric. And in spite of the pervasiveness of Christian values, when it comes to shopping and consumerism, I would argue that our nation is very un-Christian. As the following chapter will argue, our excessive shopping and materialism contrasts directly with core Christian values.

christian responses to shopping

"What does, one might say, Madison Avenue have to do with Jerusalem?"

Vincent Miller

The previous chapter examined the influence of consumerism on American society as a whole and the manner in which shopping is a reflection of our values as a society. As I have stated repeatedly, how we shop is a reflection of what we value. I am not speaking here of shopping for necessities. Instead I refer to the culture of excessive shopping here in the United States. In this section we turn to another value system: Christianity. I would like to juxtapose the broader American context above with Christian teachings. I focus on two dimensions of Christianity. The first is a selection of scriptural passages that relate directly to the practice of shopping. In my second section I turn to my own tradition, Roman Catholicism, and examine Catholic social teachings on consumerism, the economy, and consequently, shopping. Catholic social teaching represents one denomination's attempt to address through the Christian tradition the rampant consumerism of the United States.

Scripture

Throughout the New Testament we are confronted with the notion that we should not concern ourselves with matters of this world, for God will ultimately provide for us.

Do Not Worry. In Matthew's Gospel, chapter 6 has various teachings on wealth, material objects, and how they affect our relationship with the sacred. Verses 25 to 34 remind us that we should not worry about food, clothing, and the temporal in general, for God will always provide. Jesus asks, "Is not life more than food, and the body more than clothing?" (6:25). Pointing to nature, which is clothed in the glory of God, Jesus chastises humanity for the excessive and pointless worry surrounding our food, our clothing. Instead, Jesus teaches us to focus on the kingdom of God, for then all will be given to us: "So do not worry about tomorrow, for tomorrow will bring worries of its own" (6:34). Jesus is adamant in his claim that God will provide for us and that the material is inconsequential.

In a sense, a preoccupation with the material is seen to be at odds with one's focus on the sacred. Jesus challenges us in the above passage to dare to trust in God to provide for us. It would seem that if we worry too much about the here and now, we are not only redirecting our attention on fleeting, material objects but are also skeptical of God's ability to provide for us.

This idea of eternal life and satisfaction also emerges in the Gospel of John, in Jesus' encounter with the Samaritan woman. In one of my favorite New Testament passages, Jesus has a long theological discussion with a Samaritan woman drawing water from a well. Unlike the earthly water she is gathering, Jesus informs her that if she drinks living water she will never be thirsty. This living water will give the drinker eternal life (4:14). When she asks where to find this living water, he of course informs her that it comes through his heavenly Father. The Samaritan woman then asks for this water and goes on to proclaim Jesus' message to her people.

I think these two passages offer us an important message for today, especially here in the United States. At the root of the Matthew teaching is the desire for us to refocus ourselves and not to be so concerned with the objects of this world. I do not read it literally. In other words, I do not think Jesus is teaching us today merely to pray and that food and clothing will appear before us. Instead Jesus is pushing us to focus less on the material. We do not need to spend our time thinking about material objects. Instead we should center our spirituality on God. Why? The answer comes in his discussion with the Samaritan woman. Our obsession with the material, the earthly water, will always leave us wanting more. Even though that earthly water may quench our thirst, that satisfaction is only momentary, for ultimately we will become thirsty once again. Like the materialism and consumerism described above, the satisfaction we feel as a result of the material is short-lived. True satisfaction will come only if we drink from the living water. With that water, which is symbolic of a life directed toward the sacred, we will find ultimate satisfaction and we will no longer be thirsty.

> In a consumer society there are inevitably two kinds of slaves: the prisoners of addiction and the prisoners of envy.
>
> *Ivan Illich*

Mine is not a literal reading of this passage, but I do worry where a literal reading could lead in the eyes of others. I imagine that while this teaching is extremely important for us that do concern ourselves with the material world in excessive ways, there is a lesson to be learned. However, I cannot help but ask: How realistic is this for the poor? In other words, for populations that are impoverished, I am not quite sure where being told "don't worry" about food and shelter is necessarily comforting; quite the contrary.

Another interpretation could read this passage as saying the poor, because God has not provided for them, are not in God's favor. In other words, material poverty is somehow a form of punishment for them. The context in which we read any passage, including a biblical passage, will always shape how we respond to it. In spite of my concerns regarding what this message, when wrongly interpreted, could mean to the poor, these passages are significant for us today in light of our consumer culture. Jesus is saying not to focus ourselves on shopping. He is reminding us, as the previous section already indicated, that the satisfaction one feels from material goods is fleeting.

The Rich Young Man. The story of the rich young man in Matthew 19 also offers us some insight into the manner in which Jesus viewed wealth. A young man asks Jesus what he needs to do to gain eternal life. Jesus answers that in addition to keeping the commandments, "If you wish to be perfect, go, sell your possessions, and give the money to the poor, and you will have treasure in heaven; then come, follow me" (19:21). The man walked away upset, for he owned many things. This is followed by one of Jesus' most often cited statements regarding material wealth: "Again I tell you, it is easier for a camel to go through the eye of a needle than for someone who is rich to enter the kingdom of God" (19:24). When the disciples then ask for whom this is possible, Jesus says for no human, though for God everything is possible. When the Son of Man is in his glory, those who have sacrificed to follow him will receive a hundredfold: "But many who are first will be last, and the last will be first" (19:30).

I would like to spend some time unpacking this very relevant passage. First of all, this incident is often interpreted as claiming simply that Jesus hates the rich and that Christians are called to live in material poverty. Like everything in life, it is much more complex than it first appears after a cursory read. Jesus does not want anyone to be poor. Material poverty is a horrible, dehumanizing condition that goes against the full humanity of God's creation. To be hungry, to have inadequate health care, not to have access to drinkable water is not glorious. God does not want that for any part of creation. Material poverty, in fact, is an affront to God, for it denies the divine image that is equally present in all of humanity. To have such a large percentage of humanity live in poverty goes against the kingdom of God, toward which we should be working (however incompletely) here on earth. While the fullness of God's glory will never be realized in this earth, through human means in this lifetime we nonetheless must always be working toward it. When we knowingly and unknowingly act in ways that create human poverty, we are working against God's kingdom.

The passage is therefore not a glorification of poverty and a demonization of those with material goods. God does not want us to be poor. However, God also does not want our excessive materialism to go to such an extreme that it creates conditions of poverty among others. The young man is told to sell his many material goods and then give his proceeds to the poor. Only then will he gain eternal life. However, the man cannot do this; he walks away disappointed, for he has many things. It would appear from this brief encounter that the young man would prefer to have his material goods more than he would like to experience eternal life with God. He cannot sacrifice the fleeting, temporal, often meaningless objects in his life, even if in doing so he will gain the greatest gift of all: eternal life with God. While the story describes the young man as an individual who owns many goods, the man in fact appears to be owned by his material goods. They possess him, for he is unable to let them go. The promise of treasure in heaven cannot even persuade him.

How many of us are like this young man? How many of us are "owned" by our material goods? Do the many things that we buy grab hold of us in a way that makes it impossible for us to let them go? And if we cannot let them go, who really is the owner? In spite of knowing the material is fleeting, in spite of knowing that ultimately these objects do not give us the satisfaction we think we will get from them, we continue to buy and in a sense "be bought" by a consumerist culture that defines happiness by economic and material excess. The saying "he who dies with the most toys wins" comes to mind for me. In this passage Jesus is showing us another path, another option. He is showing us that true eternal life, true happiness and satisfaction, comes only through our commitment to God.

Our commitment to the sacred is reflected in our actions toward others. To quote the great commandment, "You shall love the Lord your God with all your heart, and with all your soul, and with all your strength, and with all your mind; and your neighbor as yourself" (Luke 10:27). Our relationship with the sacred is connected to our relationships with our fellow human beings. How we treat others is a reflection of how we love the sacred. You cannot have one without the other. Jesus teaches us in this passage, however, that following the commandments is not enough. Our relationship with the poor is related to our relationship with the sacred. This is an important point. Within our commitment to our fellow human beings, the poor have a privileged place. Their poverty creates an urgency within the human condition.

Within theological and ecclesial circles, the privileged place given to the poor is often called the preferential option for the poor. The preferential option for the poor seeks to call the privileged to solidarity with the poor. It calls us to choose to give the poor practical priority and shape our practice through the outlook of outcasts. We are to privilege the poor not because they are holier than us, but because they are poor. Because poverty leads to the destruction of peoples, it is contrary to the kingdom of life proclaimed by Jesus. Therefore the poor have a privileged place. In this sense, then, our solidarity with the poor evangelizes us. During the two years I volunteered at the Roman Catholic mission in Guatemala, I was surrounded by poverty. To be removed from the consumerism, and the many options prevalent in the United States, was jarring. I will admit that I wanted to shop, but I could not. I could not because it was not available to me, but more importantly I could not because I was surrounded by extreme poverty. Surrounding myself with poverty evangelized me. It made me realize that the many things I owned in fact owned me and that a simpler life in solidarity with the poor was a much more satisfying life. Sadly, it is not so easy to lead this life in the United States.

Who Is My Neighbor? Is Jesus calling us to sell everything and live as ascetics? I don't think so. Jesus does not want us all to exist in material poverty. Jesus does, however, call us who own material goods to rethink our priorities, to let certain things go, and to be informed by a life that is centered on justice to the marginalized. After all, Jesus teaches, it is extremely difficult for the rich to enter into the kingdom of God. By rich, does Jesus mean the middle class in the United States? After all, on a global scale the middle class in the United States is rich.

On days that I want to challenge myself, I say yes to this question; Jesus does mean even the middle class. Jesus is calling us to active solidarity with the poor. The word active is vital here. This is not a passive denouncement of poverty as terrible. We are being called to actively undermine structures as well as transform those everyday practices in our personal lives that create poverty. Just saying poverty is terrible is not enough. On days I am feeling less inclined to be challenged, I do not read this passage so literally. I think Jesus is calling us to be in but not of our contemporary consumer culture. There is no number or amount of goods that must be a quota for us, but instead we have to look at the principles and values that inform our lives. None of this is possible without the sacred in our lives. We cannot do this on our own, for it is impossible for human beings. Yet as Jesus teaches, with God all things are possible. This means it will not be easy. Similarly, Jesus teaches that the order of humanity will be reversed in God's kingdom. As he puts it, the last will come first.

And here we ask the question: Who is our neighbor? Too often the person we consider our neighbor is the individual who looks like us or acts like us. And for this discussion I would like to return to the Samaritan woman. Perhaps the most important dimension of this text, one that resonates with me profoundly, is that in this passage Jesus turns his ministry to those the Jews considered outsiders and enemies: the Samaritans. Jews and Samaritans did not, to put it lightly, get along. Their dispute was over the proper place of worship, since Samaritans did not recognize the Jerusalem Temple. Therefore, in this story Jesus is speaking to an unnamed woman of an enemy people. Her biological sex is also important, for Jesus not only shatters conventions in terms of ethnicity but also gender. It was inappropriate for a Jewish man to be speaking to a strange woman. Thus in his conversation with this unnamed woman, Jesus violates two social conventions. By speaking to a woman he crosses the boundary between male and female, by speaking to a Samaritan the boundary between a chosen and a rejected people.

When we are called to love our neighbor as an expression of our love of God, we are called to love that person who is not like us, even that person that maybe we have been socialized to despise and marginalize. And so the call of loving our neighbor is not just a call to reach out to the person right next to us. Instead it is truly to reach out across the chasm of difference, prejudice, and hatred in order to encounter that fellow human being who seems so different from us yet shares in our common humanity. The chasm between rich and poor is at the center of the following passage I would like to discuss, the parable of Lazarus and the rich man.

Lazarus and the Rich Man. In the parable of Lazarus and the rich man, a rich man who wore luscious purple garments and ate heartily every day is juxtaposed with Lazarus, the poor man covered in sores that would relish just one of the rich man's scraps. When Lazarus dies he is carried to the heavens by angels to the bosom of Abraham. The rich man then passes away, yet when he enters into the afterlife, he sees Abraham and Lazarus in the distance. The rich man is in torment and asks for comfort from Lazarus. At this point Abraham speaks and reminds the rich man that he received plenty in his lifetime and that Lazarus received nothing. Now in the afterlife the reverse would be true. Abraham proclaims that in addition, "Between you and us a great chasm has been fixed, so that those who might want to pass from here to you cannot do so, and no one can cross from there to us" (Luke 16:26). The rich man then begged for his living brothers to be warned of their fate through the spirit of Lazarus, for they live a similar life to his. However, Abraham refused, saying that if the brothers did not listen to Moses and the prophets, then they will not listen to the spirit of a dead man.

This parable resonates with the Matthew passage in highlighting the complete reversal of social roles in the afterlife. The rich man led a comfortable luxurious life and was never left wanting anything. Lazarus had nothing. Yet in the afterlife it is Lazarus who joins Abraham in God's glory. The rich men is left to suffer and, to add to his suffering, is able to see Lazarus. I find the distance between them and Abraham's proclamation that this chasm will be uncrossable to be an important element of the parable. In many ways, it mirrors our current gap between the rich and poor, a gap that increases every day, where the disparity between those who have in this world and those who have not only gets bigger. We should ask ourselves how we contribute to that gap, how we sleep every night in comfortable beds knowing of the suffering of others.

While Abraham depicts this gap as insurmountable, it does not have to be the case for us in this life. We live in a country where we are far removed from those who produce the goods we consume, whether they are toys, electronics, food, or clothing. They are faceless individuals in far off places. We have a vague awareness of the injustice surrounding their work. In spite of this we continue to buy and spend, supporting those companies and corporations that exploit these very workers. And we demand cheap goods. We want things that are economical, things that do not cost a lot of money. Yet for something to be cheap, it is made cheaply. Sometimes that is reflected in the quality; other times it is reflected in the labor. However, we would also be naïve if we assumed that the easy answer is to boycott goods, only support fair trade, and buy local. Because unjust or not, this cheap labor is often the sole source of income for many families that need the money desperately. So what do we do? I will return to this point in the final section, but in light of this parable I suggest one thing that we can do immediately is cross the chasm.

How do we cross that chasm? There are various ways to do it, but I am not going to write a prescription for everyone (because the way we live our lives and our financial resources differ drastically). We can all become more educated about the conditions under which our goods are made. We can recognize that our shopping habits here in the United States very concretely shape the lives of millions of individuals globally. We can admit that disposable clothing requires disposable people. These disposable people are the millions of faceless poor that make the goods that we devour and discard. We also may want to start thinking about redirecting our wealth as a nation, as a community, and as individuals in order to empower poor people and contribute to a more just world order.

> Not what you possess but what you do with what you have determines your true worth.
>
> *Thomas Carlyle*

After all, we do not want to end up like the rich man's brothers. While he begs to be able to give them a warning, Abraham wisely says that they would not pay heed. After all, they never listened before to the prophets. More importantly, if Lazarus did go to warn the brothers, would they truly have a change of heart? I suspect they would change their lives out of fear, not out of love and compassion for their fellow human being. This is an important point. I suspect that the chasm is impassable for the rich man because he cannot bring himself to cross it. He cannot see Lazarus as a full human being. The rich man is not able to recognize that perhaps he valued the wrong things in life. He does not apologize to Lazarus, and in the parable he shows no remorse. Instead he speaks of his brothers, the rich, those he identifies with as like him. He wants his brothers to be warned of their impending fate. He does not reflect any sort of conversion experience. The brothers are to be warned not so that they will live a life according to God's will because they want to and believe that is an authentic life. The warning is in order to prevent their suffering in the afterlife. If we were to transform our lives in a way that challenged the consumerist values of the United States, we should do it because we want to and are committed to do it, not because we have to do it.

A biblical passage that is important to me is the Genesis story of the brothers Cain and Abel. This is the first biblical account of murder, when Cain kills his brother Abel after God accepts Abel's sacrifice and not his own. When God goes to look for Abel and cannot find him, he asks Cain about his whereabouts. Cain responds with the famous line, "I do not know; am I my brother's keeper?" God then responds, "What have you done? Listen, your brother's blood cries out to me from the ground!" Cain's statement, the one cited more often, is significant in that it evokes that "it-is-not-my-problem" spirit that allows us to ignore the fate of millions of human beings. However, it is what he doesn't say—or I should clarify, what he doesn't hear—that I find more compelling. As God exclaims, his brother's blood cries out from the ground. God tells him to listen. It is the deafness, that inability to hear the blood of his brother shrieking in agony, that stays with me when I read this biblical narrative. It forces us to come to terms with the times we have turned a deaf ear to the suffering of humanity. The story reminds me of when I ignore the cries of innocent victims of injustice and do nothing to challenge the status quo. The narrative is also a harsh reminder of the daily slaughter of our human brothers and sisters by each other and that this tragic tale repeats itself daily.

The Sheep and the Goats. Returning to the Gospel of Matthew, perhaps no other passage is more often cited concerning our obligation to our neighbor as an expression of our solidarity with the poor as is the end of Matthew 25 that discusses the sheep and the goats. Often, though, the passage is quoted without any mention of the sheep and the goats. Usually citations begin with verse 23, which is a litany of ways in which the behavior of the righteous can be described: "For I was hungry and you gave me food, I was thirsty and you gave me drink, a stranger and you welcomed me, naked and you clothed me, ill and you cared for me, in prison and you visited me" (Matt. 25:35-36). The righteous are confused at this and ask Jesus when they literally did these things for him. Jesus then answers, "Amen, I say to you, whatever you did for one of these least brothers of mine, you did for me" (25:40). I have seen this passage at campus ministries on Roman Catholic college campuses. I have seen it on brochures and pamphlets for workshops on social justice. It is a beautiful passage, one that I remember very clearly loving as a child. Yet it is not the full story.

The passage actually begins with: "When the Son of Man comes in his glory, and all the angels with him, he will sit upon his glorious throne, and all the nations will be assembled before him. And he will separate them one from another, as a shepherd separates the sheep from the goats" (25:31-32). The sheep are on the right and represent the righteous. Jesus then moves to the above-referenced speech (25:23-40), which is where folks often end the story. But if you continue reading, Jesus then turns to those on his left, the goats, and proclaims, "Depart from me, you accursed, into the eternal fire prepared for the devil and his angels" (25:41). The reason given is that they did not do any of the things that the righteous did for others. They ask the same question that the righteous asked, wondering when they did not reach out to Jesus. He responds that when they did not reach out to others, they were also denying him. Jesus then condemns them to eternal punishment, and the righteous to eternal life.

I have thought a lot about why this passage often appears edited. The fuller version poses a much stronger challenge to us. The abridged version also leaves us with a warm feeling, knowing that if we reach out to others we are in fact reaching out to God. There is no judgment in the abridged version. The full passage talks about judgment and condemnation. It seemingly speaks of a God who condemns others. This idea is difficult for us to reconcile with the Christian notion of a God who is all forgiving and all loving. Within Christianity the idea of Jesus sending the accursed to eternal suffering seems at odds with the redemptive suffering of the cross, the God described in the parable of the Prodigal Son, the God who will always welcome us home. After all, God's offer of grace and love is never rescinded; God loves us unconditionally.

I do not read this passage as one of God condemning us. I read it as a passage that describes how we condemn ourselves. Jesus is trying to teach us that our love of and devotion to God is so inextricably linked to our love of and commitment to others that it is one and the same. When we reach out to the poor and the marginalized, we are reaching out to God. When we ignore human suffering and turn a blind eye, we are rejecting God. Ultimately, Christians imagine the afterlife as union with the sacred, an eternal life of bliss. Yet we have to want that union. God does not force us to be in God's presence. God does not force us to love God. That is a choice we all make. Jesus proclaims that when we reject and ignore the marginalized, we are rejecting God, thus choosing not to be in God's presence. Those who are condemned chose to be condemned. They have chosen to ignore human suffering, they have chosen to ignore the sacred in their lives, and now they are no longer at God's side by their choice.

Like the rich man's brothers, we cannot be motivated by fear. We cannot read biblical passages such as the ones

I have cited and live a life of solidarity in order to prevent our alienation from God. We have to want it authentically in our hearts, and that demands a true conversion. This will have concrete implications for how we view ourselves, others, and the way that we act. Acting out of fear is not authentic, and frankly, God will see right through us. Ultimately, you live a lie if the motivations behind your actions are not authentic. Fear cannot be that which calls us to justice, but instead, solidarity, compassion, and love for our fellow human beings.

The Prodigal Son. The story of the Prodigal Son can also shed some light on this discussion. In that parable, Jesus describes two sons that are given an inheritance by their father. One son takes the money and runs. He spends it frivolously. The older son stays at his father's side. When a famine hits the region, the younger son decides to return to his father's side. He goes with the commitment of working for his father in order to earn his keep. Before he can get the words out, his father sees him from a distance and immediately runs to embrace him. He orders a fine robe for his son and orders a feast. Upon hearing this, the older son is bitter, for he has remained beside his father and has never been treated so luxuriously. To that his father replies, "Son, you are always with me, and all that is mine is yours. But we had to celebrate and rejoice, because this brother of yours was dead and has come to life; he was lost and has been found" (Luke 15:31-32).

The story of the Prodigal Son is ultimately a story about God's love, forgiveness, and eternal offer of grace. The father in the story represents God and the sons humanity. Even though the younger son spent all of his money and left his father's side, his father forgives him. In fact, his father not only forgives him but rejoices in his return. This does not take away from the love he has for his older son, who always remained with him. Nonetheless, the father in this parable is truly moved to have his son return asking for authentic forgiveness. All biblical passages that speak of our condemnation should be situated in light of this divine forgiveness. We condemn ourselves when we turn away from God. We are the ones that alienate ourselves from the sacred. God will always welcome our return with eager and open arms.

The Beatitudes. I cannot write a section on the poor and consumerism without mentioning the beatitudes. The central teachings of Jesus' Sermon on the Mount, the beatitudes, stress the theme of the reversal of the world order that has been highlighted in other New Testament passages. The beatitudes open with the blessings that the downtrodden and the despised will have in the kingdom of God: "Blessed are you who are poor, for yours is the kingdom of God. Blessed are you who are hungry now, for you will be filled. Blessed are you who weep now, for you will laugh. Blessed are you when people hate you, and when they exclude you, revile you, and defame you on account of the Son of Man. Rejoice on that day and leap for joy, for surely your reward is great in heaven" (Luke 6:20-23). The poor will be rich, the hungry will be satisfied, and the marginalized will be placed at the center. Their suffering will not continue on into eternity; there is relief in sight in the afterlife.

However, for those on the other extreme, the fate is much more uncertain: "But woe to you who are rich, for you have received your consolation. Woe to you who are full now, for you will be hungry. Woe to you who are laughing now, for you will mourn and weep. Woe to you when all speak well of you, for that is what their ancestors did to the false prophets" (Luke 6:24-26). Those of us living in the United States may feel a bit of a jolt when reading these verses. Not that everyone in the United States can be considered rich. But we live in a rich nation where an overwhelming number of the population would fall on the "wealthy" side of the global economic spectrum. We put ourselves in the position of the "wealthy" when we ignore the unjust suffering of others and turn a blind eye to how we contribute to the exploitation of our fellow human being.

Relating to the Sacred. How does this impact our shopping? I cannot tell you how much to shop, where to shop, and when to shop. I can ask you, however, to ponder why you shop. Do we fill voids in our lives with material goods? Do we define our self-worth by what we own? If this is the case, which I think it is for the dominant American society, then the poor rate very low in terms of individuals that we as a society collectively value.

And here the biblical teachings cited above play a significant role. The rich man valued his wealth and his comforts. He valued his brothers and wanted to prevent a similar fate happening to them. He did not think of Lazarus. He expressed no compassion for the difficult life Lazarus led and how much he suffered. This is ironic, for at that very moment the rich man was suffering the pain that Lazarus had experienced throughout his lifetime. And yet the rich man does not identify with Lazarus, even though he, unlike his brothers, at that moment can relate to his pain in ways that his brothers could never fathom. The rich man, even at that moment, cannot see Lazarus as his equal. Our excessive consumerism has implications for both how we view ourselves and assess our self-worth as well as how we view and value those around us.

Similarly, when Jesus teaches us that God will provide for us, he is also calling us to refocus our attention away from materialism and toward our relationship with the sacred. Our relationship with the sacred is defined by how we relate to our fellow human beings. It relates to how we shop and how we value shopping in our lives. A few months ago I was driving a colleague to a dinner party with my family. As we drove by the local mall, my two-year-old recognized it and exclaimed its name. My colleague, a fellow shopper, laughed and exclaimed, "Well we know whose kid this is." I laughed nervously along with her, yet part of me felt anxiety and shame.

As I mentioned in the previous section, in the United States we are defined by shopping. It is a national pastime. In the name of research (because serious academics do not have time for television), I recently watched an episode of *Oprah* on the culture of spending in the United States. Families were challenged not to spend any money for a week or weekend. Other families were challenged to spend less, to cut out dining out, and to decentralize consumerism in their family lives. For the families that have young children, this was devastating for the kids. It amazed me to see how early on in life children are shaped by consumerism. A report on the *Today Show* highlighted a study of children and brand recognition. Ten-year-olds could recognize brands that their parents could not. Early on our children are indoctrinated into the gospel of shopping.

The one beacon of light in the *Oprah* episode was that, after the days or weeks or even months with a life that was not defined by shopping, many of the families were happier. They were spending more time together, connecting in ways they had not when consumerism ruled their lives. This is an important dimension to add to our discussion of the implications of consumerism. Shopping affects how we value ourselves. Shopping concretely affects the lives of others who are the faceless masses that produce the goods we consume. Shopping also has an enormous impact on the individuals who are part of our intimate lives. Our shopping reveals a value system to our friends, families, and loved ones. For parents it teaches our children what is important, what they need in life, and how they define their happiness. Do we really need so much? There are television shows that force people to de-clutter because their homes are filled with piles of stuff that they have accumulated. What sort of values do we teach future generations when we spend more than we should and buy more than our living spaces can accommodate?

The Acts of the Apostles depicts an early Christian community radically different than Christianity today: "All who believed were together and had all things in common; they would sell their possessions and goods and distribute the proceeds to all, as any had need" (Acts 2:44-45). We can deduce from this passage that the members of early churches did not own private property. If this was not the case for everyone, it was certainly the practice of some and the expectation for others. It is clear that participation in the early church meant some sense of renunciation of personal goods.

Economy and Environment. The renunciation of private property is not a realistic option for Christians in the contemporary United States nor for churches in this country. Our economy today does not exist in such a form that would make this possible. But we can rethink the amount of goods we accumulate, the mass quantities of things that we purchase, and whether we need so many privately owned goods. Our money could be redirected elsewhere. We also could attempt to spend that money more wisely, or save it, or use it to support organizations that do solidarity work with marginalized populations. Parishioners could collectively pool their resources in order to aid with the maintenance of their churches instead of using church funds for everyday tasks. These funds could then be redirected to support ministry in the community. While the renunciation of private property is an unrealistic goal for contemporary American Christians in our capitalist economy, it can still inspire us to challenge why we allow ourselves to get caught up in the consumerist circle of excessive spending.

> Once again, we come to the Holiday Season, a deeply religious time that each of us observes, in his own way, by going to the mall of his choice.
>
> *Dave Barry*

Our fellow human being is not the only dimension of this world that is affected by our consumerism. The very earth is endangered by our practices. And in abusing the earth we are again affronting God, for part of our role as God's creation is to protect this planet. Genesis teaches us that the earth belongs to God and that we are its caretakers: "Be fruitful and multiply, and fill the earth and subdue it; and have dominion over the fish of the sea and over the birds of the air and over every living thing that moves upon the earth" (1:28). We do not own the earth. It is not ours to consume and exploit. Yet that is what we do, consume and exploit the resources of the planet as if they are ours and as if they have no value. We are only one element of God's creation. Everything God makes is seen as good. Therefore we are commissioned to respect and care for it.

When humanity is placed in the Garden of Eden in the book of Genesis, we are placed there to take care of it. We are caretakers of God's creation. God creates the earth, yet there is no one there to take care of it. So humanity is created, a humanity that emerges from the dust of the ground. One question often raised by theologians with environmental concerns is whether the first chapters of Genesis reveal a positive or negative attitude toward creation. I argue that Genesis is ambivalent. On the positive side, God as creator implies ownership. We humans are merely stewards, and creation is not ours. Creation, as I stated above, is good. In naming us caretakers or stewards of this earth, God has entrusted us to care for creation. We are different; we are created in God's image. That image should inspire us to care for the earth with the same love and respect we expect from God. It does not give us full license to destroy the earth.

Sadly, there are some negative implications to the Genesis accounts. For many, the responsibility of dominion and stewardship gives humanity full warrant for exploitation. In other words, our care for the earth means that the earth is here to serve us. In a similar vein, the creation accounts in Genesis set humanity apart from the rest of creation. Too often we easily interpret being set apart or distinctive as entirely different and better. The fact that humanity is created in the image of God, one of the most beautiful notions in the Hebrew Scriptures, has been misinterpreted by some to mean that we somehow are more valuable than the rest of creation. The image of God is misconstrued to legitimize the abuse and disregard of the earth. We have to remember that we are part of creation and creation is part of us.

While theologians often speak of anthropology, the study of the human being and our relationship with the sacred, we should also speak of cosmology, our relationship with all of creation. We cannot understand the human as separate from the rest of the earth. The image of God in us does not give us a pass to abuse and mistreat creation. It does not give us full reign on God's earth. In many ways, we should treat the earth in the same way that we would want to be treated. Theologically, the emphasis is on the integrated, interconnected nature of all of creation, arguing against an individualistic, autonomous understanding of the human. This is a model grounded in solidarity, stressing the diverse yet interdependent nature of all of creation. Humanity needs to come to terms with its interrelationship with and dependency on the rest of creation.

Our consumerist excesses in the United States are destroying our planet. We consume at the expense of our fellow human beings, this earth, and future generations. Here in the United States, we consume a disproportionate amount of the world's resources with little regard to how our consumption affects others. And often when awareness is raised, individuals scoff at scientific research that proves to us that we are abusing our planet. We have done a terrible job of caring for this earth, putting our needs before the needs not only of the rest of humanity but also the planet, God's creation. In the first chapter of Genesis, God looked at creation and saw it as good. Does the way we voraciously devour the world's resources imply that we see goodness and value in it?

Christian Social Teaching

My presentation of Christian values thus far has focused on the ways in which Christianity is in many ways against the tide of the capitalist consumer economic and cultural ethos that dominates the United States. Ironically, some scholars have argued that Christianity is not only a kindred spirit to capitalism but has contributed to the rise of capitalism. For Max Weber, a Protestant (and particularly Calvinist) ethic was behind the rise of capitalism. He begins with the Protestant notion that we show our devotion to God through our hard work. Diligent work becomes a sign of God's grace.

Roman Catholicism, on the other hand, is otherworldly. Catholicism, at least until the late twentieth century, focused on being not of the world. Unlike Catholicism, Protestantism gives value to worldly activity. From this emphasis on hard work as a sign of God's grace came the idea that accumulating capital is a duty in and of itself. In capitalism, profit is an end in itself and is seen as virtuous. Calvinists saw worldly success as a clue to whether or not you were saved. Profit and material success became a sign of God's favor. This religious attitude paved the way to modern capitalism. Weber concluded that Protestantism is one contributing factor of capitalism.

While I do not want to vilify Protestantism as the root religious cause of capitalism, the United States is a nation founded on the values of Protestantism. Roman Catholics have not played a definitive role in the dominant ethos of this country. This may change as Hispanics continue to increase in numbers, a population that is overwhelmingly Catholic. It is perhaps because it has not been the dominant denomination, and admittedly that it is my own tradition, that I turn to the Catholic social teachings as a body of Christian writings that address shopping and consumerism within a Christian framework.

Homeboy Industries. For three years I lived in Los Angeles and taught at Loyola Marymount University. After living in Los Angeles for a few months, I began to hear about a Jesuit named Greg Boyle. "You have to meet him," people kept telling me. "He works with Latino ex-gang members." Finally after over two years, I brought a group of students to the offices of Homeboy Industries, located in Boyle Heights, one of the most violent areas in Los Angeles. Previously, Father Boyle was Pastor of Dolores Mission Church. Dolores Mission is the poorest parish in the Los Angeles Catholic Archdiocese. The parish is compromised of the largest public housing developments west of the Mississippi (Pico Gardens and Aliso Village). These housing projects have the highest concentration of gang activity in the entire city.

Homeboy Industries is an employment referral center and economic development program for at-risk and gang-involved youth. While pastoring at Dolores Mission, Father Greg, or G as his homies affectionately call him, witnessed the violent gang activity that was destroying his neighborhood. After months of saying funeral masses for the children in his midst, Greg decided to do something about it. He founded Homeboy Industries, a sort of gang rehab, to help young men and women who wanted to leave gang life. A huge problem Greg noted was the inability for ex-gang members to find employment, especially if they had juvenile or prison records. A central dimension of Homeboy Industries' work is their job referral program, which also includes job readiness, job training, and even buying clothing for the ex-gang members to wear to interviews and work. They also offer free tattoo removal of gang tattoos, a service that has a nine-month waiting list. Homeboy Industries also runs various businesses: for example, a bakery, silk-screening, merchandising, and graffiti removal. Over one thousand gang members, looking to leave the cycle of violence and poverty, visit Homeboy Industries monthly.

I have heard Greg speak of his ministry, and I do not dare attempt to put his moving words into my own. What has always amazed me about Greg is his ability to see the full humanity of young men and women who are seen as the refuse of our society, forgotten youth often described as animals. I once heard Greg say, "I have stopped trying to be as holy as the people I serve." I was moved to tears by his radical testimony, for he finds worthiness in those seen as unworthy. Greg always brings some of his homies with him when he speaks, and I remember talking to one of them, a twenty-one-year-old, about the weeks he spent in solitary confinement while serving time for a violent crime. We were standing outside a rather fancy reception the University held for Greg, and this young man was clearly uncomfortable with his surroundings. It turned out that he had never set foot on a college campus. At twenty-one, I had graduated from Georgetown University.

Latin American liberation theologians speak of the preferential option for the poor, calling us to view the world through the eyes of the poor and privilege their perspective in our lives. It is grounded in a Christian vision of humanity where the last comes first. Greg Boyle lives the preferential option for the poor. He also lives in a state of voluntary poverty, a notion Asian theologians have developed in order to speak of the renunciation of privilege that can empower those without privilege. When you go to Homeboy Industries, you do not hear much Christian language, yet the vision, the mission, the very impulse behind this organization is Christian. Standing in Homeboy Industries you are confronted by the radical call of Christian discipleship. You see the church in a forgotten space, an undesirable space, and you see the church being truly church. Like the woman's witness in Samaria, Greg Boyle and Homeboy Industries is a witness of the church not just on the boundary but having crossed the border to minister in a space inhabited by the undesirables of society.

Catholic Social Teachings. When I think of Catholic social teachings, I think of Greg Boyle. Catholic social teachings (hereafter CST) are known as the Roman Catholic Church's best kept secret. CST focus on the intersection of faith and everyday life. At the foundation of CST is the Catholic notion of the common good. The common good teaches us that we are social in nature and thus interdependent. We do not exist as highly isolated individuals. Instead we exist as the community that is humanity. The foundation of the common good is the Genesis notion that we are all created in the image and likeness of God. Yet God in the Christian tradition is triune. Therefore our *imago Dei* is in the image of the Trinity. The Trinity reveals a God that is one but threefold, a God who is constituted by the relationships between the three persons of the Trinity. Relationality is that which reflects the image of God within us. It is through our relationships that we most concretely reflect God's image.

A trinitarian understanding of the divine image is grounded in historical Christian theology. The Trinity is not self-contained but instead flows into the economy of creation and salvation. The doctrine of the Trinity also becomes the foundation for Christian understandings of community and consequently of church. The mutual, relational love of the Trinity as expressed through the Christ becomes the foundation for an egalitarian understanding of our relationships and their formalizations within community.

Our *imago Dei* (the image of God within us) is found in the relational nature of who we are as human beings. Through our relationship with God, our fellow human beings, and the rest of creation we reflect the image of God within us. The human being is not self-contained but instead is constituted by relationships. This is not an uncritical and romanticized understanding of relationships. Not all relations reflect the image of God. Instead, relationships are judged against the norm of Jesus' concrete life, ministry, death, and resurrection. Through our mirroring of Jesus' justice-infused ministry, we grow in the image of Christ and consequently the image of God. Hierarchical relationships that privilege certain sectors of humanity are deemed unrevelatory, for they contradict Jesus' inclusive vision of community. Within CST, therefore, human salvation is social. The common good highlights this communal model. Therefore, our personal salvation is inextricably linked to the salvation of all of humanity. We cannot understand our salvation without connecting it to the salvation of others.

From the foundation of the common good spirals out a morality that is the foundation of CST. After all, the belief that we are social in nature has moral implications. Three significant themes emerge from the morality of the common good. The first is rights and duties. Because CST have a communitarian basis, their morality believes in the positive obligation toward others. Often when we hear the words duty or obligation, we think of things that we "have" to do. This is not the attitude CST embrace. Our obligation toward others is something we want to do. We want to be in solidarity with our fellow human being. We want to empower them. We embrace the fact that our love of God is reflected in our love of neighbor. This positive obligation is not only at a personal level but also at a societal level. Civil, political, and economic rights entail duties—duties of solidarity toward others. Regarding private property and consumer society, the CST claim that you can earn what you want; what is important is how you use your wealth. There are many extremely wealthy individuals who use their wealth in positive ways and not just to accumulate consumer goods.

A second theme that emerges from the morality of the common good is subsidiarity. The principle of subsidiarity regulates how institutions interact with each other in their solidarity work. In other words, this principle embraces the idea that any work that can be done by a smaller organization rather than a larger, more complex organization should be handled by the smaller. Subsidiarity is about decentralizing power so that more than one group is in control.

Peace, understood as right relation with God and one's neighbor on a global scale, is the third theme that emerges. The foundation of peace in CST is the just war theory. This theory defines war as an aberration that can be justified only by a theory of exceptions. You may be asking yourself, what does war have to do with shopping? Economic, social, and cultural inequalities threaten peace. There is a direct correlation between poverty and violence.

See, Judge, Act. This Roman Catholic worldview promotes a communal understanding of the human. A primary emphasis of these social teachings is the intersection of faith and everyday life. Their method is characterized by three moments: "see, judge, and act." They counsel us to assess, theologically judge, and then respond to the struggles and concerns of the world around us. On the more institutional or hierarchical level of the church, Catholic social teachings are found in official documents written by bishops or the Pope. These documents address a particular social issue and offer theological reflection in light of Catholic teachings.

> One can buy anything with money except morality.
>
> *Jean-Jacques Rousseau*

They also include a call for action. The birth of this tradition is firmly situated in the 1891 papal encyclical *Rerum Novarum*, which dealt with the question of workers' rights. If you read this document, you find a Catholic call for a fair wage for workers and an affirmation of their rights. The document *sees* the late-nineteenth-century context of industrialization, urbanization, and poverty; *judges* the mistreatment and unjust conditions of workers in light of their full humanity as God's creation; and calls for the *acts* of workers' rights. *Rerum Novarum* created a new genre of church writings as the first social encyclical. When it was released many felt the Pope should not comment on issues such as workers' rights. Though shaped by their historical era, these documents deal with timeless struggles. The CST, in addition to the common good, advocate for the dignity of the human person and protect the poor and the environment.

In the context of shopping, CST demand the question, "When is enough *enough?*" In a recent document, *Centesimus Annus*, John Paul II writes, "It is not wrong to want to live better; what is wrong is a style of life which is presumed to be better when it is directed toward 'having' rather than 'being' and which wants to have more not in order to be more but in order to spend life in enjoyment as an end in itself" (no. 36, all papal documents are found on the Vatican website: vatican.va). This is a fundamental point. John Paul II is reminding us that we should not feel guilty about wanting to live a good life. Reading the parable of Lazarus and the rich man and the story of the young rich man should not make us feel guilty about wanting to provide for ourselves and our families. What is wrong, as he so eloquently puts it, is a life dominated by "having," a life controlled by the desire to possess material objects and accumulate as much as possible. Instead, the Pope argues, life should be enjoyed in and of itself. Our lives cannot be valued or our happiness measured solely on the basis of material wealth.

In the same section the Pope continues, "It is therefore necessary to create lifestyles in which the quest for truth, beauty, goodness, and communion with others for the sake of common growth are the factors which determine consumer choices, savings, and investments." This is yet another significant point. John Paul II is arguing that our theological worldviews should inform our consumer choices. The very same principles that define our relationship to the sacred define our relationship with material goods. Notice that the Pope is not arguing against spending money, saving money, or investing money. He is not calling for the renunciation of material wealth. He is, however, saying that we are to embrace a spirituality of economics that guides how we value and spend our money. While for many shopping is a type of spiritual experience, the type of spirituality the Pope says should infuse our shopping is quite different from the "high" one can feel from a purchase.

Catholic social teachings are critical of most of the economic models that dominate the global landscape. They condemn socialism because socialism, CST claim (though this is disputed), denies private property and encourages class struggle. On the other extreme, however, CST condemn capitalism because it denies the common good and the human dignity of the worker. Capitalism, as viewed by this tradition, values economic profit over human life and also focuses too heavily on individual economic success. A system based on the accumulation of personal wealth can never be based on the common good of the human community. In this system one's own personal gain is always at the forefront. As I have highlighted repeatedly, American consumerist culture places the consumer before the worker. Therefore, the dignity of the worker does not play a significant role in capitalist culture. Now one might say that this is not true, that in the United States there are unions and laws to protect workers' rights. This may be true. However, so many of the goods we purchase are produced and cultivated by foreign workers that we do contribute to their labor conditions and their diminished dignity whether we are aware of it or not.

Justice and Charity. Consumption in and of itself is not sinful. The problem is excessive consumption. Catholic social teachings suggest that extra wealth should be put at the service of the poor. Excessive consumption is environmentally destructive, and treating consumption as a goal in life denies human dignity. Consumption is destructive to the environment and to ourselves. I will return to the environmentally destructive nature of our excessive consumption shortly. Needless to say, we in the United States consume at a rate that is destructive to the planet. Catholic social teachings do not condemn the individual who has excessive wealth. They do, however, challenge us to redirect our wealth in solidarity with the poor. Similarly, when shopping becomes the center of our lives, our fellow humans fade into the background.

The 2009 papal encyclical by Pope Benedict XVI, *Caritas in Veritate*, is the most recent document in the Catholic social tradition. The foundation of this document is the intimate connection between justice and charity. Justice is intrinsic to and inseparable from charity (6). "Charity in truth, to which Jesus Christ bore witness by his earthly life and especially by his death and resurrection, is the principal driving force behind the authentic development of every person and of all humanity" (1). Charity to our fellow human being is the foundation of our relationship with the human community. The foundation of charity is the truth of God's salvific message through Jesus. "Without truth, without trust and love for what is true, there is no social conscience and responsibility, and social action ends up serving private interests and the logic of power, resulting in social fragmentation, especially in a globalized society at difficult times like the present" (5). The Pope's comments on love connect to our earlier biblical discussion on intention. Our actions should emerge from love and compassion for our fellow human being, not out of fear of condemnation. When we do not feel authentic love for our fellow human being, when we do not see our fellow human being as our equal, as our brother and sister, this is when it becomes easy to devalue human beings over material goods. Ultimately, this desire for the common good is at the foundation of justice and charity.

When our goals and values are distorted, when shopping becomes more important than being with our fellow human being, when profit becomes a goal in itself, it allows us to become accomplices in the creation of global poverty. Development should be reevaluated through the lens of the common good. Development needs to be integral; economic and technological development is not enough. "It is therefore necessary to cultivate a public conscience that considers food and access to water as universal rights of all human beings, without distinction or discrimination" (27). In other words, it is easy to speak of the greatness of the human race when we see all our technological advancements and progress. However, when we take into consideration the growing global poverty in this world, the growing chasm between rich and poor, it is very difficult to see ourselves as an advanced human culture. What kind of advanced culture knowingly devalues the majority of the world's population as less important than consumer goods?

A fundamental problem, the encyclical argues, is that humans think they are the author of their own lives. This stems from our original sin. We do not want to admit that we need God in our lives in order to behave justly toward each other. An example is given in the Pope's discussion of the contemporary marketplace. The economic market is not unjust in and of itself, but certain ideologies can make it destructive. Economics is not ethically neutral; the economy needs ethics. Here in the United States we have become well aware of that, with the major economic scandals of the past decades and the excessive spending of executives in a time when the economy was plummeting. Businesses, Benedict XVI argues, need to have more social responsibility. Too often they outsource their labor to other companies to get themselves off the hook. Yet they have a responsibility to every worker that is somehow connected to their work. Similarly, as this lengthy quote elaborates, the consumer has a social responsibility:

> Hence the consumer has a specific social responsibility, which goes hand-in-hand with the social responsibility of the enterprise. Consumers should be continually educated regarding their daily role, which can be exercised with respect for moral principles without diminishing the intrinsic economic rationality of the act of purchasing. In the retail industry, particularly at times like the present when purchasing power has diminished and people must live more frugally, it is necessary to explore other paths: for example, forms of cooperative purchasing like the consumer cooperatives that have been in operation since the nineteenth century, partly through the initiative of Catholics. In addition, it can be helpful to promote new ways of marketing products from deprived areas of the world, so as to guarantee their producers a decent return. However, certain conditions need to be met: the market should be genuinely transparent; the producers, as well as increasing their profit margins, should also receive improved formation in professional skills and technology; and finally, trade of this kind must not become hostage to partisan ideologies. A more incisive role for consumers, as long as they themselves

> are not manipulated by associations that do not truly represent them, is a desirable element for building economic democracy. (66)

In other words, we cannot place responsibility on those who produce the goods we buy; the buyer is also responsible. We have an obligation to educate ourselves regarding the implications of our consumerism.

With the Internet and the endless access to information we have in this day and age, it is difficult for anyone to claim ignorance. Similarly, we can rethink the way we spend our money and find more collaborative ways to share goods in a communal manner in order to reduce our individual mass consumption. We can use our power as consumers to encourage those businesses who do have just labor practices. The consumer has an immense amount of power to influence corporations; after all, the market caters to us. If consumers in the United States would take a stand on behalf of workers' rights, if we would claim that cheap goods are not worth cheapening fellow human beings, then maybe we could use the power of our dollars to transform the world. However, the business cannot be taken off the hook. "Even if the ethical considerations that currently inform debate on the social responsibility of the corporate world are not all acceptable from the perspective of the church's social doctrine, there is nevertheless a growing conviction that business management cannot concern itself only with the interests of the proprietors but must also assume responsibility for all the other stakeholders who contribute to the life of the business: the workers, the clients, the suppliers of various elements of production, the community of reference" (40). The bottom line cannot dominate business practice. Instead, the dignity of the human person defines how we produce and how we consume.

Prosperity Gospel

Not all Christians would agree with my arguments in this book. Some would say that God is not only in favor of consumerism but that, in fact, one's wealthy excesses demonstrate that one has gained God's favor. The prosperity gospel movement is an example of this marrying of consumerism and Christianity. Proponents of the prosperity gospel preach that if you are faithful to God and donate generously to your church, God will reward you financially. Many see their wealthy preachers with their many material excesses and think that their success is a reflection of God's grace upon them. Therefore, they see following a preacher or a movement as a way of hopefully gaining favor themselves. These pastors flaunt their wealth, encouraging their followers to support them financially so that God will also put them in their favor.

The prosperity gospel (also known as the "health and wealth gospel") ultimately argues that God does not want Christians to be poor. Adherents believe that God has promised the true followers prosperity in this life and that this prosperity is revealed through the acquisition of material goods. A central Scripture passage in this movement is John 10:10: "I came that they may have life, and have it abundantly." This passage is interpreted as justifying mass consumption and ultimately shopping. The movement is growing tremendously in the United States and abroad. The four largest megachurches in the United States include the prosperity gospel as part of their theology. The prosperity gospel teaches fundamentally that since God created the material world, God wants us to enjoy that world. Similarly, they argue that God does not want us to be poor.

However, in casting material wealth as a sign of God's favor, the prosperity gospel inadvertently vilifies the poor. Taken to the extreme, the prosperity gospel represents the marriage of massive American consumption and Protestant Christianity. Perhaps this is its appeal and why it is spreading so rapidly in the United States. Prosperity preachers evoke images of Old Testament figures Solomon and David and their riches to legitimize their teachings. And while Atlanta-based Creflo A. Dollar Jr. (his real name) claims that his prosperity gospel does not have to do with material wealth, he owns two Rolls Royces, a private jet, and million-dollar homes in Atlanta and New York. Some prosperity preachers link entrepreneurship with the biblical message, offering business courses through their churches. Followers see the wealth of their pastors and assume that they too will have all the riches and designer goods their religious leaders do if only they follow the "Christian" way and donate to their churches. The prosperity gospel justifies the wealth of many individuals and gives the poor the hope that through their faith they will one day be wealthy. God will provide for them eventually, if they remain faithful to their pastors and donate to their churches.

This chapter has focused on Christian resources for beginning to recast the way we shop. I have argued throughout this section that fundamental Christian values are very much in contrast to the way that we understand and are dominated by consumerism in the United States. While shopping is not sinful, valuing those things that we shop for more than we value fellow human beings,

God's creation, and our relationship with the sacred is sinful. We cannot allow shopping to define who we are and how we engage the world. Yet we exist in this world, and more importantly we exist in the United States (though the United States is not the only country dominated by consumerism). In the final chapter, I offer my reflections on how we can shop and still be Christian. This is not a how-to guide on how to live your life. But I hope that my struggles and ponderings on this topic can help inform you in the everyday shopping that saturates our lives.

3

a christian reconfiguration of shopping

And why do you worry about clothing?

Matthew 6:28

I teach a course every other year entitled Religion and Gender. In the course, a group of undergrads and I spend the entire semester focused on Genesis 2–3, the story of Adam and Eve, sometimes referred to as the fall of humanity. We do a close read of the text and then examine how Muslims, Christians, and Jews have interpreted this passage throughout history. We conclude with the implications of Adam and Eve for our understandings of gender roles both historically and in the contemporary era. Every semester I teach this class, I get a fresh perspective on the story, primarily through the eyes of the twenty-year-olds who read the text with me.

One element of the story always stands out to me and is always inevitably raised by the students: the question of nudity. After all, prior to their fall, "the man and his wife were both naked, and were not ashamed" (Gen 2:25). In fact, one of the first things Adam and Eve do after they have eaten the forbidden fruit is to put on clothing. Prior to their transgression (I call it "transgression" because the passage never mentions the word "sin"), they are happy and naked. They are not ashamed of their bodies and they are not ashamed to be naked in front of each other. I think about Adam and Eve when I look at my two boys, ages two and four, who love to run around the house naked and are not ashamed of their bodies. I think about the fact that symbolically, clothing is a result of our disobedience of God, our desire to be like God. Is fashion, like the pains of childbirth and the forced labor over the land, yet another consequence of sin? If that is the case, as I stare at my closet, that is one consequence I have thoroughly embraced.

In many ways the rampant consumerism of the United States today is a fairly recent phenomenon, at least in contrast to the early Christian foundations of the United States. There is a puritanical thread in American culture that is very much anti-consumerist. Nonetheless, as a result of advances in technology and the effects of globalization, consumerism and the United States now go hand in hand. Shopping is a national pastime. I would even push this point further and say that shopping is an element of American nationalism. To be a good "American" you have to shop. But to be a good Christian you have to think carefully about how and why you shop. The topic of how Christians can live in this culture of shopping and remain true to their Christian values is the topic of this final section. Ultimately mine is a constructive proposal that I hope can give you insight into the everyday practice of shopping and its implications for Christian life. What and how we consume is a reflection of our relationship with the sacred, our relationship with others, and our relationship with ourselves.

In this final chapter, I hope to find a balance and not fall into the many extremes we have discussed throughout the book. I do not want to claim that materialism and shopping are a directive from God and that our wealth is a reflection of God's favor. I also do not want to claim that we have to be world-denying and that material objects represent an uncontrollable temptation we are obliged to avoid and master. We cannot go to the extreme of anti-materialism, but we should have an awareness that there are ethical implications to our consumerism and that what we buy and how we buy has an impact on others. We need to cultivate a sense of sufficiency and adequacy in light of material possessions and recognize that there is beauty in the material world as a reflection of the goodness of God's creation.

Christianity and Anti-Materialism

It is easy to interpret Christianity as being anti-materialist. Passages such as the following support such claims:

> Do not love the world or the things in the world. The love of the Father is not in those who love the world; for all that is in the world—the desire of the flesh, the desire of the eyes, the pride in riches—comes not from the Father but from the world. And the world and its desire are passing away, but those who do the will of God live forever. (1 John 2:15-17)

Ultimately, this passage speaks to the finite nature of all the material goods and excesses of this material world. It tells us not to lust after such things, for they impede our relationship with the sacred. First John does not claim that these material things are evil. However, the passage warns us of the ways in which we can get caught up in the fleeting materialism of this world rather than the eternal life and love of God.

It reminds me of Jesus' comment to the Samaritan woman, that the water of this world will always leave you thirsty but that the living water of God will leave you eternally satisfied. These passages do not present the material world as evil, but they do point out that it can be tempting. We can be distracted easily by this world and forget that our focus should always be on the sacred.

Perhaps no other Christian thinker has addressed this topic more readily (and I should add influentially) than Augustine of Hippo, the great North African church father. Augustine of Hippo, born in 354 in Thagaste (in modern-day Algeria), was arguably the most influential theologian in the history of Christianity. Considered the "father" of the doctrine of original sin, Augustine's monumental corpus covers a variety of themes, including the Trinity, grace, sexual ethics, the nature of the church and spirituality.

I always say shopping is cheaper than a psychiatrist.

Tammy Faye Bakker

Augustine's *Confessions* is considered the first Western spiritual autobiography. The first paragraph of *Confessions* contains probably one of my favorite lines in the Christian corpus: "Our hearts are restless until they rest in thee." With these simple lines Augustine argues that we are made for God; we are created in order to praise God. And since we are created for God, we will find peace only in God. The longing and dissatisfaction we humans feel is because we are created in the image of God yet due to original sin are incomplete without God. Sin is the state in which we are born, due to the fallen state of humanity. Augustine traces this fallen state to the Genesis account of Adam and Eve. Because Adam and Eve sinned, all of us are born in a state of sin. Augustine was the first Christian thinker to elaborate the doctrine of original sin, the Christian idea that all of humanity is born in a sinful state as a result of our parents' arrogant disobedience. We have no control over this. While we are created in God's image, that image is distorted. Christian thinkers have interpreted that level of distortion in varying degrees over the history of Christian thought.

You may be wondering how Augustine defines sin. Sin is turning away from God and seeking pleasure in others. What has this text taught us about some Christian attitudes that we find in Augustine? For Augustine, we humans feel longing and dissatisfaction because we are created in the image of God but remain incomplete without God on account of our sinfulness. Sin is a result of human freedom. Because God has given us the gift of free will, we have the option to turn away from God. That option can result in sin, the rejection of the sacred in our lives.

In Augustine's worldview, which is consequently the dominant Christian worldview, original sin creates a human state where we are inclined to sin because of our corrupt human nature. In a sense our choice is predetermined, to choose to turn from God rather than embrace God. Perhaps it is outdated or even false, but the doctrine of original sin is central to Christian beliefs. Original sin is the basis of belief in Christ's redemptive work: Jesus takes away our original sin. It is through God's grace mediated through Jesus' redemptive work that our corrupt human nature is transformed to being inclined toward the sacred. This doctrine explains the origin of evil and the need for salvation. It also justifies the need for the church as mediator of Christ's healing. Unfortunately, the one question not answered by this doctrine is why we alienate ourselves from the divine. Ultimately, original sin argues that evil is a part of our world prior to our own personal choices and decisions.

Augustine does not resolve the tension between Adam being created wholly oriented toward God and the resulting question about the source of his sin. We never receive an explanation of why our first parents chose to turn away from God instead of following God's will. This is especially perplexing given that, if we are created in the image of God, we are fully oriented toward God. Many theologians over the years have described Adam and Eve's first sin as pride. This egoism is what led our first parents to want to be like God and eat the fruit. Sin damages the image of God within us, yet grace heals us. Medieval theologians will argue that original sin represents what was lost to sin in our nature; therefore we inherit a defected human nature, not the created one. Baptism infuses us with grace, thus healing our nature. But we are permanently scarred by disordered desire (our punishment for original sin) even after original sin is removed.

Shopping as Concupiscence

We are not the way God intended us to be. Humanity, like all of God's creation, is good, for how could a God that is all-good and all-loving create anything but a good creation? Yet while God created us good, our original sin has clouded that goodness. Because of that distortion, when it comes to the material world, we are often misguided toward it. A theme that emerges in Augustine's corpus is how we have misguided desire, or lust and passion, in relation to the material world and other human beings. How does Augustine define lust and passion? He often describes it as concupiscence: strong desire, especially sexual, that sometimes implies sin or evil. Concupiscence refers to compulsive and pleasureless enjoyment. Augustine sees all desire as dangerous and evil, for passion leads to a loss of control.

When I teach about concupiscence in my classes, I always use food as an example. Pizza and Hot Tamales are often mentioned. I am a self-confessed pizza-terian. What does that mean? That means that I can eat pizza at every meal. But that is not the problem. The problem is how much pizza I eat when I eat pizza. I can never just have one or two pieces. I have to eat three or four. And frankly, by the third piece I am usually no longer tasting the pizza but robotically shoving it in my mouth. I am no longer enjoying the pizza. In fact I am well aware that I am going to be sick from the pizza, but I keep eating. The same can be said of Hot Tamales. I can never have one or two handfuls. I always finish the box. This pleasureless, compulsive experience is what Augustine is talking about when he describes concupiscence.

Augustine himself speaks of food in his discussions of concupiscence. Perhaps one of the most famous and one of my favorite passages in *Confessions* is his account of stealing pears from a pear tree as a teenager with his friends. Why did they steal the pears? Not because they needed them. In fact, the fruit was not that desirable and they were not going to eat it. Instead, Augustine writes, they stole for the pleasure of the act itself. In other words, it was not the desire for the pears themselves that motivated them but the thrill of stealing. Augustine does not blame the pears for this. He is clear that the pears are not that appealing and that they end up feeding them to pigs. Therefore, it is not the material good that is seductive. The pears, after all, are God's creation. Instead it is the act and thrill of stealing that tempts them.

These misguided desires impede our relationship with the sacred. When Augustine speaks of the thrill of stealing, he could also be describing sexual lust. For the purposes of our book, he could be discussing shopping. Compulsive shopping is a massive problem in the contemporary United States. Many individuals shop just to shop. Many do not even wear or use the many things that they purchase. Instead, they are seduced by the thrill of the new purchase and all that it promises. Of course there is an entire consumer industry that wants us to feel this way. Consumerist culture thrives on it. So we find individuals here in the United States with massive debt who continue to spend, continue to buy things even if they do not have room for their purchases—all for the thrill of shopping.

Individuals who shop compulsively think that what they buy will somehow make them feel better and improve their lives. This is far from the case. Shopaholics often describe getting a rush or high from the act of shopping and "crashing" in anxiety once they realize all that they have spent and the debt they have incurred. Shopaholics often hide their purchases and are ashamed to have even their loved ones see how much they spend. Compulsive shopping is an addiction that has been compared to alcoholism and gambling. The shopper cannot control what he or she spends and often does not even use what he or she spends. We are a nation of shoppers that enables shopaholics. Shopping is a national pastime. In the United States, what we buy, what we wear, and what car we drive are means of self-expression. People are incapable of controlling their urge to spend, which can lead to destructive behavior. Today in the United States, shopping is a form of concupiscence.

For Augustine, the answer to the destructive cycle of concupiscence is equilibrium. Material objects are in no way evil and tempting in and of themselves. It is not the object that is the problem but the misdirected desire for the object. And too often in our shopping we end up using rather than enjoying things. I think Augustine would agree with me when I say that consumer desire today is a form of concupiscence. We have this insatiable desire for material goods that can never be satisfied, and often it is the act of shopping, not what we purchase, that is so appealing to us. Our passion for material objects becomes a vicious cycle that we want to avoid and we never find pleasurable. Shopping becomes a meaningless act that dominates our lives, in very destructive ways for some.

Curiously, there is one strong similarity between the compulsive desire that dominates consumerism and core Christian values. Both teach that material objects will never ultimately satisfy you. Consumerism seduces us constantly, giving us new objects to desire, so that we are never satisfied with what we have. Christianity warns us that this will always be the case, for we are looking for satisfaction in the wrong places. Both consumerism and religion say that objects cannot quench our desire. Consumerism, however, is much more flighty—in consumerism the pleasure is in the desire, not in the object itself.

The first epistle of Timothy reminds us of the futility of the constant desire for material goods:

> For we brought nothing into the world, so that we can take nothing out of it; but if we have food and clothing, we will be content with these. But those who want to be rich fall into temptation and are trapped by many senseless and harmful desires that plunge people into ruin and destruction. For the love of money is a root of all kinds of evil, and in their eagerness to be rich some have wandered away from the faith and pierced themselves with many pains. (1 Timothy 6:7-10)

This passage reveals that the slogan "whoever dies with the most toys wins" is a lie. Eternity, for Christians, is absent of material possessions. We enter this world with nothing material and we leave in the same way.

This letter warns us of the perils of this consumerist concupiscence. We need to stop obsessing about what we own and what we don't own and instead focus on those things that have true value in our lives. This passage also implies a point that I have highlighted earlier, that our obsession with material goods can be destructive not only to ourselves but to others as well. I am referring not only to those personal relationships that can be impacted when one overshops, but also to those faceless workers who suffer creating the very goods we consume. Love of money is the "root of all evils" because it deludes us into putting material objects before human beings, before ourselves, and before our relationship with the sacred.

Excessive shopping can lead to financial and personal destruction, yet in many ways this is acceptable in American culture. I have always wondered how it is possible that we live in a world where buying things we cannot afford is now normative. I often think sadly of individuals who buy things on sale because it is a great price. Yet they buy these things on credit cards, and ultimately the interest will make these items even more expensive than their original price. And yet people continue this vicious cycle of credit card debt, paying only the minimum, watching their debt grow. Proverbs reminds us that "the borrower is the slave of the lender" (Proverbs 22:7). And here I am not speaking of the shopping addict. This is the common reality for many individuals in the United States and globally. Living well beyond one's means has become normative.

> Whoever said money can't buy happiness simply didn't know where to go shopping.
>
> *Bo Derek*

The Shopper

We need to focus on what shopping does to the shopper. Our value and our authority do not come from material goods. Success is not defined by the amount of money we make. The things that we should truly value in our lives are not those things that have monetary value. Money, ultimately, will not give us the type of authentic satisfaction many of us want in our lives. How we spend our money is a direct reflection of how we respect ourselves.

I had my first job when I was fourteen years old. I began washing dishes at the local pizza joint. I hated that job. I also felt like I really should not have to work, since my parents could afford otherwise. Yet through encouraging me to work, my parents taught me a valuable lesson: to respect money, especially the money I made. It was much more difficult for me to waste money that I earned scraping dirty pizza pans than it was to waste money my parents handed over to me.

We are seduced easily by the cheapness of goods. Why are we more eager to buy a dress that is reduced from two hundred to one hundred dollars than a dress that is one hundred dollars from the start? The marked-down dress is a bargain; the hundred-dollar dress is not. And if there is something we in the United States love, it is a good bargain. We will drive miles to outlet malls to get a good deal, even though the money we spend on gas and the time we spend driving to these often inconvenient locations probably outweighs the money we save on purchases. We buy cheap goods knowing that their quality is going to be questionable, that they may be disposable.

This does not only apply to clothing. In my sophomore year of college, my parents took me to IKEA, a beacon of cheap and stylish furniture, to buy a bed and bookshelves. I was thrilled with them after the three hours it took us to build them. And at the end of the year, knowing I was going to spend my junior year abroad, I had to get rid of the bed and bookshelves. So what did I do? I left them outside the townhouse my friends and I were renting, knowing full well some other college students would pick them up. The furniture had been purchased so cheaply that it was not worth the effort of trying to sell it. Similarly, even though one would think I would be attached to the first bed I owned as an adult, I was not. It was a cheap, white, metal IKEA bed. In contrast, I still own my first twin bed, an antique purchased for me when I was six years old.

It is ironic that in the era of cheap goods, many of our necessities in life keep increasing: gas, food, health care, education, and housing. It would appear that we are being suckered. The consumerist economy increases our access to cheap goods, making us think that life is getting cheaper, yet the major expenses in life keep increasing exponentially. I am also particularly concerned with cheap food. Cheap food requires cheap labor. It can also lead to relaxed standards of hygiene and quality. The amount of cheap processed food that is consumed in the United States is alarming.

When I finished my master's degree at age twenty-three, I was tempted for a moment to forget a PhD and move to Latin America to work with the poor. That was a dream of mine. I had been and continue to be extremely influenced by Latin American liberation theology, a theological school that places the poor at the center of Christian faith and life. Latin American liberation theologians argue that God has a preferential option for the poor. These theologians also challenge us to put the poor first.

This challenge does not mean merely acknowledging the horrors of global poverty. That is not enough. Saying that poverty is awful, being horrified at the extent of global poverty, does not help poor people. Thinking Angelina Jolie, Brad Pitt, Wyclef Jean, and Bono are cool for helping poor people or watching the Live Aid concert is not enough. Buying a red iPod or Gap t-shirt is not enough. I find the connection between charity donations and consumerism in the United States to be especially disturbing. We need to buy in order to give.

We have become too complacent in our acknowledgment of the evils of this world, as if this recognition is enough. It is not; in fact it does not even come close. Instead, Latin American liberation theologians challenge us to engage in concrete action in solidarity with the poor. We need to do something. In fact, they will argue, unless we do something we are not being authentic Christians.

Being a good Christian does not merely entail regular church attendance and prayer. Nurturing a personal relationship with God and a communal spirituality are central to Latin American liberation theology as well, but they do not suffice for any Christian. Genuine Christian life includes concrete social justice in solidarity with the poor. Indeed, if we do not engage in such action, we are not being true Christians.

I often teach courses that focus on the teachings of Latin American liberation theology. I am always surprised at the manner in which my students respond to these teachings. Many Christian students are surprised and pleased at the presence of such a strong call to action and appeal to solidarity with the poor within their religious tradition. They resonate strongly with the biblical teachings highlighted by Latin American liberation theology. They usually interpret it as the way Christianity should be, nodding eagerly at the preferential option for the poor and condemnation of the rich in these texts. When we read the Exodus story, the quintessential story of God's solidarity with the oppressed within liberation theologies, the class practically cheers for the Hebrew slaves. And yet they do not realize that they are the Egyptians in the story. Students want a religion that cares for the poor, but they do not live their lives in that manner. They do not want to recognize that they are the rich.

Why are they the rich? They are the rich because they sit in air-conditioned classrooms and complain about having to read and study so much. They do not understand their education as a privilege and a gift. In many of their worlds, a university education is an expectation that they sometimes engage reluctantly. It is not surprising to me that my poorer and working-class students often that take their education more seriously. With wisdom well beyond her years, a young woman I taught who worked from midnight to eight in the morning would go home to shower and show up at my 9 a.m. class. This student, who had candidly shared with her classmates her financial struggles one day, shocked us all later in the semester when she wisely claimed, after losing her job, "I am broke but I am not poor, because I am here." It was a jolt to the middle-class students who constantly complained about being "poor."

This is not the only reason I classify them as rich. They are rich because they are unaware of how the lives they lead and the lives many of them will lead are interconnected with global poverty. Those who become aware often do not think that this complicity applies to them. In many ways they remind me of Lazarus and the rich man. The rich man's sin was his blindness to poverty. He walked by Lazarus everyday but never truly saw him. The poor were nonexistent to him. And this is what amazes me with many of my students (and frankly most educated liberals I know). They can somehow claim solidarity with the poor, they celebrate that solidarity, but they do not in any way shape their everyday practices to reflect that solidarity. They do not see themselves in any way complicit in the web of global poverty. But we all contribute to the global consumerist culture built on the broken backs of the poor, whether or not we accept this fact. It is very difficult to make the jump from the everyday to the structural. So we think that if we are not personally "oppressing" the poor, we are off the hook. Yet the everyday is the foundation of social structures.

Is Shopping a Sin?

So the question, of course, is whether shopping is sinful. The simple answer is no, shopping is not sinful. We have to shop. Without shopping we would be unable to obtain the basic necessities in life that sustain us. However, when we allow shopping to rule our lives, when it comes to define who we are and how we relate to the world, then shopping can be an indicator of our misguided values. Figuring out when one has crossed the line, when one has allowed for shopping to become excessively important in one's world, is extremely difficult. There are no easy answers here and no blanket decision or proscription. The intention of this book is not to provide self-help for individuals who are worried about their shopping habits. The remainder of this book will focus on attempting to answer two questions: Is all frivolous shopping sinful? If not, when does shopping become sinful?

One answer comes from Catholic economist John A. Ryan (1869–1945), who argued that superfluous wealth goes against our commitment to our neighbor. He did not, however, advocate poverty, but instead suggested that one live a comfortable but not excessive life. He argued for a redistribution of power and wealth on behalf of the most marginalized within the capitalist system. For Ryan, it is not wrong to want to live a comfortable life. However, excessive wealth should be directed toward the poor. Ryan's proposal, while idealistic, may seem unrealistic to many today. Or is it? Would it be that hard to imagine spending less money on one's material excesses and directing some of that money to solidarity work? It does not have to be only about money. Our time is a valuable commodity. How much time do we spend shopping? Could that time not be focused on volunteering, community service, and church-based initiatives?

This solidarity, at its best, emerges from right intentions. Galatians gives insight on this point: "They asked only one thing, that we remember the poor, which was actually what I was eager to do" (Gal 2:10). This poetic verse reminds us that our commitment to the poor emerges from our positive obligation toward others. Our obligation to our neighbor cannot be something we are reluctant to embrace. It should emerge out of love for our neighbor as an expression of our love of the sacred. Humanity was created with the gift of free will—so we can choose to love God and not be forced to. Similarly, we are given the choice to open our hearts to the sacred.

In the Christian worldview, all of creation reflects the glory of God. For Augustine, created things are to be used, but only God can be enjoyed. We are not to get pleasure from the material world because the temptation to become obsessed with the material world is too great. Remember, for Augustine it is not material objects that are somehow corrupt or sinful. It is our unhealthy connection to them. The temptation of the material world often spirals into concupiscence, into an insatiable desire that can never be quenched. To contextualize it in terms of shopping, the concupiscence of shopping is revealed when we shop just for the sake of shopping. We are never satisfied with what we own and instead move fervently from one item to the other. It is not what we buy but buying that becomes the problem. This Augustinian take on shopping sounds eerily similar to the description of American consumerism I outlined in the first part of this book. It would appear that in the dominant American ethos, shopping for the sake of shopping is normative and acceptable.

The result of this obsession with the act of shopping is that it becomes the center of our lives. Our time and energy are focused on consumerism. And if we focus on this, that means we are ignoring a plethora of other things. For Jesus, detachment from the material is necessary for attachment to him. In other words, we cannot serve God and money. If money becomes how we define our lives, if our material goods become the indicator of how we value the worth of others, then we cannot also be leading a Christian life. This goes entirely against the central teachings of the prosperity gospel. Grace is not having things, it is what we do with the things we have. In other words, our material wealth, for those of us that are privileged to have it, is not a reflection of our favor in the eyes of God. Instead, it is what we do with our material wealth that is reflective of our authentic Christian values.

Within the Christian framework, to live a life governed by materialism is to live a life we were not created to lead. I go back to the sense of restlessness Augustine evoked in his *Confessions*. Christianity teaches us that we will always be left wanting, always be unsatisfied, if we allow anything but our relationship with the sacred to govern our lives. We will continue to drift from one unfulfilled desire to another because our desires are misdirected. Only when we focus our desire on that which we are created to desire—God— will we find true satisfaction and contentment in life.

In the Oprah episode I mentioned earlier, one family was highlighted where the parents were hoarders. They had tons and tons of the same one item, mostly because they had been purchased on sale, with a coupon, or because it was cheap. The mother, who did most of the shopping, spoke of the time and energy she spent scouring deals and clipping coupons. It consumed her life. I watched in horror at a pantry that had stockpiled enough food to feed ten families for almost a year. And then, unsurprisingly,

I thought of Scripture: "Do not store up for yourselves treasures on earth, where moth and rust consume and where thieves break in and steal; but store up for yourselves treasures in heaven, where neither moth nor rust consumes and where thieves do not break in and steal. For where your treasure is, there your heart will be also" (Matt 6:19-21).

This passage from the Gospel of Matthew seems a direct contrast to the saying that the winner is the one who dies with the most goods. Matthew is reminding us that we cannot spend our lives focused on accumulating material goods. The stockpiling of them and the protection of them will come to dominate our lives. I am not critiquing the act of cutting coupons, taking advantage of a bargain, and looking for sales. I am, however, commenting on the danger of these behaviors becoming a way of life that leads to an unhealthy focus on shopping and saving, so much so that you end up spending more because of perceived savings.

I have a lot of stuff. I would be lying to you if I said I did not. I didn't always have a lot of stuff. I lived for two years on two suitcases worth of clothing and a few boxes of books. I remember living in Guatemala and watching ads for items on television attempting to seduce me into purchasing them. And yet I could not. In my neighborhood there was no Target, no major department store (the city was two hours away). I cannot describe to you the almost serene sense of relief I felt in being unable to purchase something. I suppose I could desire it, but there was very little I could do about it.

This is a radically different context from the contemporary United States. The Internet has revolutionized shopping. If we have the money and the access (and by access I mean access to a computer and a reliable mail carrier) we can have almost anything in the world sent to our homes. We do not have to do anything more than type and click. Sometimes I think we shop because it is so easy for us to shop.

This reinforces the Augustinian read of consumerism as concupiscence. We shop because we can, and we often do not even enjoy it. Similarly, technology has created yet another barrier between human contact and shopping. Shopping is now entirely depersonalized. I have very clear memories of how personalized shopping was, with my parents when I was a child in the early 1980s. We would go to the neighborhood drugstore where folks had accounts on good faith that they would pay monthly. The pharmacist knew everything about our family. We would then go to the hardware store where everyone knew my parents' names and had a sense of their household issues. When my mother would go shopping for clothing it was almost a ritual between her and the sales associates. It was a personal relationship with personal interaction. I remember that our local toy store owner knew every toy we owned because my parents bought all of our toys there throughout our childhood. As a child I loved to read, and I remember the thrill of going to the bookstore, thumbing through books, and deciding which one I would read that week. My parents did not spend excessive amounts of money to receive this personal attention. This was the way people shopped.

How do I shop today? I no longer go to the local pharmacy or toy store or hardware store. Even though my

> There must be more to life than having everything!
> *Maurice Sendak*

parents still live in the same place and I live very close by, all of those businesses have closed, replaced by larger chains that take us fifteen to twenty-five minutes to get to by car. Why would I go to the local drugstore, even if it is a chain? I can order from drugstore.com and get free shipping and no tax. Who has time to go to a bookstore and look at books? They are cheaper online anyway and I can read other people's reviews—people I do not know and have never met—in order to decide whether I want to purchase a book. Why go to a toy store? You can comparison shop online. I am not claiming that some of this technology is a bad thing. Comparison shopping, becoming an educated consumer, and the general access to information that technology has given us is commendable.

Technology, though, brings the world together while also keeping us physically apart. Technology can give us a false sense of intimacy that is no replacement for embodied human interaction. Let's take Facebook as an example. I am not on Facebook and have no intention of joining. My friends and students complain about this constantly. I have been called anti-technology and a Luddite. Trust me, anyone who shops online as much as I do (since I am always so busy working to make money to spend) is not anti-technology. The thing that bothers me most about Facebook is the category of "friend." You can "friend" strangers, send them messages, develop relationships with them. These are people you may never have met in the flesh and have no intention of meeting. I am in my mid-thirties and use the term "friend" sparingly. I have many acquaintances in my life, but if you were to ask me who I consider my friends in this world, I would list fewer than ten people. Were I on Facebook, I could have hundreds of "friends." I am not critiquing Internet social networking, but technology has created a sense of intimacy that can never and should never replace our flesh-and-blood relationships. The Internet depersonalizes intimacy. It does so with our shopping. In the United States we are now removed not only from the people who create and produce the goods we buy but also now from those who sell the goods.

Shopping, like eating, drinking, and having sex, is not sinful in and of itself. If we are going to define sin as alienation from God, when an everyday behavior comes to consume our lives in unhealthy ways, then a reassessment of our values and a consideration of whether these behaviors are impeding the things we truly should cherish in life is beneficial. When I mention alienation from God, however, I am not speaking exclusively of an individualistic relationship between God and the believer. As the various biblical passages from the previous chapter clearly express, our relationship with the human community is an expression of our love of God. We cannot have one without the other. We exist in this world, and the way we act toward all of God's creation is a sign of our relationship with God. The way we exist in the world, our everyday practices, are a reflection of our internal values. Or are they? Can we judge a book by its cover? What is the connection between appearance and value?

Fashion and the Incarnation

If you have not gathered by now, I have a love-hate relationship with fashion. I hate that I love it. I am well aware that the fashion industry is a capitalist machine that tries to convince me every season that my entire closet is out of style and that I need to revamp my entire look or I am going to appear horribly frumpy. I know that they are constantly thinking of ways to tempt me. Stores such as Zara, I have learned, set their stock based on their clients' shopping patterns in each location. I receive emails from online vendors with suggestions based on my previous purchases. Big Brother is definitely watching. And yet, I truly believe that a beautiful dress is a work of art. I do see fashion as an art form. I am also well aware that my attention to my appearance impacts my life in both negative and positive ways. I also think about shows like *What Not to Wear* and how some individuals who have gone through difficult times feel truly transformed by a change in wardrobe and hairstyle.

I do pay attention to how I look. Sometimes that works in extremely beneficial ways in my career. Students like that I am "hip," ask me about my clothing, and this makes me immediately more accessible to them. As part of a profession of notoriously bad dressers, among college professors I stand out as more polished. I often get asked by my colleagues, "Why are you so dressed up?" I am dressed up because I love to dress up (ironic since I was a tomboy who as a child ripped ribbons out of my hair). I am dressed up also because I want to appear professional to my students. Teaching is, after all, a job. My dress has helped me in situations where I have dealt with nonacademics. However, my love of fashion has also impacted me negatively. Women who pay attention to their appearance are often categorized as frivolous and unintelligent. A woman that cares about how she looks does not care about anything else. Care for one's exterior is stereotyped as behavior at the expense of the interior. Women are expected to "dress like men" in order to be taken seriously by the workplace. This was the mantra of the early feminist movement. We were encouraged to mask our femininity in order to exist in a man's world.

If one Scripture passage could condemn my interest in fashion, it is found in 1 Timothy: "Women should dress themselves modestly and decently in suitable clothing, not with their hair braided, or with gold, pearls, or expensive clothes, but with good works, as is proper for women who profess reverence for God" (1 Tim 2:9-10). I will admit that this is one of my least favorite passages in the New Testament, not just because it appears to critique my love of fashion but also because it is followed by proscription limiting the apostolic authority of women. This passage needs to be contextualized. The author's critiques arise over concerns regarding a group of preachers who were challenging the leadership of the church. In other words, the statements in 1 Timothy should not be interpreted as timeless claims over women's behavior as a whole. Biblical teachings, especially those that directly address the cultural specificity of their era (in this case, dress codes), are to be read in light of the context in which they were written.

Shopping and the Body. For many women, in addition to dealing with negative stereotypes about their attention to their appearance, we also struggle with the sexualization of our bodies and the role clothing plays in that. After all, our clothing reveals as it conceals. As Christians we are part of an extremely twisted, hypocritical, and misogynistic tradition when it comes to bodies in general and women's bodies in particular. We are part of a religious tradition that celebrates the incarnation, yet through the centuries the body is presented as an impediment to our relationship with the sacred. For women our bodies historically have been the barrier between us and the priesthood, and in the words of some theologians such as Augustine, our ability to authentically reflect the *imago Dei* as women. Whether Christianity is reducing us to mothers or to objects of sexual and moral temptation, the Christian tradition does not promote a healthy understanding of the body.

Feminist theologians highlight the body as a site and expression of our relationship with God. Recovering the body is a central feminist theological task. This recovery is nuanced by an acknowledgment that when the female body is the focus of theological reflection, this body is often reduced to sex. So the female body is emphasized in terms of biological reproduction and consequently motherhood, or the body becomes sexual temptation. Feminists, therefore, want to overcome this dualism and present female bodies as an authentic reflection of our image of God and a means of expressing our relationship with the sacred.

Within popular culture perhaps no other artist has been so celebrated by her body in the past decade than Jennifer Lopez. As a fellow Latina and fellow shopper, for years I have been fascinated by the emphasis on Jennifer's body in general and on her "butt" in particular. When she first exploded onto the scene, it seemed like the only thing people could talk about was Jennifer's butt. Her body and not her talent, her ability to dance, act, and sing, nor even her face mattered. Everyone wanted to talk about her body, and more specifically her butt.

Lopez's body is a public site where Latina sexuality and Latina bodies are constructed, exploited, and celebrated. Even though Lopez has undergone a radical transformation since her earlier career, appearing much leaner and blonder than she did in the mid 1990s, her body remains foundational to her success. Lopez made a name for herself in her adamant rejection of idealized Hollywood body types and her very public celebration of her buttocks. Jennifer's celebration of her "big" butt, which represents "normal" everyday Latinas, is slightly ridiculous in light of the fact that Lopez is much smaller than the average woman in the United States. Also, given that her butt shrank as her fame grew, it is clear that she was not always entirely comfortable with her curves. To embrace the butt and the body is an empowering act. In celebrating the butt one rejects the demonization of the butt. However, in our celebration of the body, we cannot reduce the body to a sexualized object.

The Incarnation. The celebration of the body is a fundamental dimension of fashion and, I would argue, a fundamental aspect of Christian belief, though it appears in ambiguous guises. At the heart of my claim is the incarnation. And to begin our discussion on the incarnation I would like to turn to the second century c.e., specifically to Irenaeus of Lyons, whom some call the first Christian theologian. Born between 140 and 160 c.e., Irenaeus is most known for his writings against Gnosticism (one of many early Christian movements that was eventually condemned as heretical). Due to this, many of his writings are polemical.

A key concern for Irenaeus' theology is the question of God's universal salvific will, or in other words, God's desire to save all of humanity. Irenaeus describes humanity as created in the likeness of God but having lost something in the fall. Jesus as the son becomes the archetype of likeness, which is revealed in the incarnation. We humans lost our resemblance, but our resemblance is reestablished by the incarnation. Irenaeus' notion of likeness is dynamic.

For Irenaeus, likeness has to do with human behavior; it is a soteriological (or salvific) notion. At times Irenaeus also speaks of similitude. Similitude has to do with our similarity to God. Image and similitude reveal something about human nature. Likeness is a soteriological concept that refers to the human's relationship with God.

Irenaeus does not refute the notion that the Son has always existed with the Father. Important, however, is the role of the incarnation within salvation history and its implications for our creation in the image and likeness of God. Christ's incarnation was necessary, for human beings could not save themselves from sin; they needed Christ. The manner in which Christ saves is connected with the importance of obedience in Irenaeus' theology. Jesus' obedience did away with Adam and Eve's disobedience. Incarnation is the central point in human history.

In Irenaeus, the image of God refers to the body and soul, while the likeness refers to grace dwelling within us. Before the fall, Adam and Eve possessed the image and were children in spirit. They were supposed to move on to spiritual maturity. When they sinned they lost God's spirit and thus their likeness to God. Christ restores our spirit through his restoring of our communion with God. Our salvation is the recovery through Christ of what was lost in Adam, namely the image and likeness of God. The Son reflects the image of God and we in turn are the image of the Son. Until the incarnation, the image of God was invisible. Jesus Christ makes visible the invisible God.

God and Fashion. You may be wondering what all this theological jargon from the second century has to do with fashion and the body. The reason I mention Irenaeus is that he reveals the importance of Jesus' body, his incarnation, early on in Christian history. Jesus saves through his embodiment in the human body. Jesus' body is fundamental to our salvation. And if Jesus' body is fundamental to our salvation, then our bodies are as well. It is through the body, and not in spite of the body, that we are saved. In addition, as part of God's creation, the body is good.

This is an important point. The body cannot be reduced to an impediment of our salvation. Too often it is. Christians have a love-hate relationship with their bodies. On the one hand, we affirm the importance and goodness of the bodies. On the other hand, we constantly are juxtaposing the body and the soul. The body is depicted as the source of temptation. We cannot be too attentive to the body, or focus too much on the body, or worry too much about what we put on our bodies, because doing so will jeopardize our holiness. In a sense, the Augustinian warning of the excesses of the body has been assumed to mean that the body is the problem.

But Augustine never vilifies the body. His concern is our inappropriate emphasis on all things body related. Holiness is often defined as denial of the body. In a sense, attention to one's body is interpreted as lack of attention to "important" matters. The sign of a holy (and frankly, at times, an "intelligent") person is one who does not pay attention to their body and their appearance. This conflicts with the Christian belief that the body is good, that creation is good, and that even Christ was incarnate in a historical human body.

The condemnation of women's ornamentation is cited often to promote modest dress among women in particular. And yet the ambiguity surrounding Christianity's relationship with the body is also revealed in Christianity's attitude toward dress and fashion. Clearly Christianity and fashion have a relationship, for if they did not we would not have clerical dress. Fashion is not frivolous entirely in the Christian worldview. What do I mean by Christian fashion? In various instances we find dress as a fundamental expression of Christian identity and authority. One has only to look at clerical vestments. In some denominations certain colors have ritual significance. In many of

> Anyone who lives within their means suffers from a lack of imagination.
>
> *Oscar Wilde*

the churches where clergy wear vestments, especially in middle-class and upper-class communities, the embroidery and craftsmanship that goes into stoles and other vestments is extremely intricate. The clerical collar is a crosscultural signifier of Christian authority. Christianity is not the only religion that connects fashion with authority within their traditions. Dress matters in religious ritual.

As a child I hated having to wake up early on Sunday mornings and put on a dress for church. It seemed like an unnecessary hassle. A theologian even as a child, I would mentally construct arguments that God did not care what I wore, that appearance was not important. I truly did not understand why people "got dressed up" for church. It made no sense to me. Now as an adult I sit in church surrounded by shorts, jeans, and flip-flops. I wear dresses and skirts. Why? Not for my love of clothes but as a sign of respect. In the same way I want to look professional at work, I want to look respectful at mass. I admit that, even though I live in Miami where it is hot out, those shorts and jeans trouble me.

I am not alone in wanting to put on a dress for church. In fact in many ways, I am on the low end of the church fashion spectrum. In many Christian denominations, elaborate dress is a fundamental aspect of church life. This is particularly the case in many Pentecostal denominations such as the Church of God in Christ. Often the elaborate dress of a woman is a clear indicator of her authority within ecclesial settings. Respectable dress is not a plain blouse. These very elaborate suits and dresses often contain embroidery and beading and are expensive. Clothing becomes a marker not only of one's social status but of one's role in the ecclesial setting. In certain Christian churches, proscriptions on women's dress also included whether or not makeup was acceptable and how they wore their hair. Appearance and sanctity go hand in hand.

Underlying the relationship between appearance and holiness, whether it is a clerical collar or an ankle length skirt, is a theology that claims that one's outward appearance and how one constructs that appearance through fashion are indicators of one's commitment to the sacred. Therefore, the ornamentation (or lack thereof) of the body can be more than a negative indicator of one's holiness. To return to the Vincent Miller quote cited earlier in this book, Madison Avenue does have something to do with Jerusalem, and it is not always negative.

Faith and fashion in some circles go hand in hand. For women in particular, restrictions on their dress were not always oppressive. They were able to transform many of the limitations placed on them and become powerful leaders in their churches. Religion, culture, power, and clothing intersect through women's dress. This has been seen recently in the arrest of Sudanese female journalist Lubna Hussein for wearing pants. Islamic law stated that she could receive up to forty lashes for her immodest dress. International uproar over this led to her punishment being reduced to a fine of two hundred dollars. She refused to pay the fine and was imprisoned, later to be released. She insists upon wearing pants, which have been interpreted as immodest dress for women under Sudan's Islamic law. Clearly, even today, the clothing we choose in our everyday lives are a religious and political act.

Beauty. There is actually a field in the study of theology that directly connects fashion and faith. That area is called theological aesthetics. Theological aesthetics is a growing area in contemporary theology. Though not necessarily a theological "school" or "field" per se, those authors working on theological aesthetics constitute a conversation or particular theological style grounded in their concern with beauty. Theological aesthetics holds that in the encounter with beauty there is an experience of the divine. This emphasis on the aesthetic is based on the idea that within the realm of symbol, imagination, emotion, and art one finds a privileged expression of the encounter with the divine and its articulation.

Theological aesthetics serves as a corrective to the highly textual approach of theology, which often does not incorporate the fullness of humanity's encounter with God. The emphasis on the metaphorical and poetic, however, does not come at the expense of the metaphysical. Instead, theological aesthetics argues that beauty is a transcendental attribute of God; as such, beauty is an aspect of God's revelation. Theological reflection on beauty should therefore incorporate aesthetic expressions of the human encounter with beauty's revelation.

Taking seriously theological aesthetics, the idea that beauty is an attribute of the sacred, opens up a lot of doors for theological resources. These include the more "academic" sources of literature, art history, architecture, and musicology. To link shopping, consumerism, and aesthetics for example, one could look at the elaborate ornamentation of churches accompanied by the artifacts that are sometimes sold in them. You can go shopping at church. Further examples are found in fashion, popular culture, popular music, and so on.

You may be saying that to speak of beauty in this day and age seems in many ways absurd. What some hold as "beautiful" is really a subjective opinion. "Beauty" understood in a transcendent manner as a core attribute of the sacred does not exist. When I speak of God's beauty, however, I am not reducing that to what humans see as beautiful or alluring. In fact for Christians, in many ways one of the most beautiful sights is Jesus' suffering face on the cross. The "ugliness" of the cross paradoxically reveals God's glory through the path of humiliation. We cannot have the resurrection without the cross, and it is through the ugliness of Jesus' suffering that the beauty of God's love for us is revealed.

Ultimately, an emphasis on aesthetics pushes us to see outward appearances as containing theological value. Is there a theology behind fashion? I would argue that there is and that a theology of fashion recognizes that there is value to the material. There is a relationship between one's appearance and one's values. If we are going to argue that how we shop is a reflection of what we value, then what we put on our bodies is a reflection of how we see ourselves and how we want to present ourselves. I am not recommending that we judge a book by its cover, but we also cannot dismiss exterior appearances. As the letter of James reminds us,

> My brothers and sisters, do you with your acts of favoritism really believe in our glorious Lord Jesus Christ? For if a person with gold rings and in fine clothes comes into your assembly, and if a poor person in dirty clothes also comes in, and if you take notice of the one wearing the fine clothes and say, "Have a seat here, please," while to the one who is poor you say, "Stand there," or, "Sit at my feet," have you not made distinctions among yourselves, and become judges with evil thoughts? (James 2:1-4)

This sort of superficial judgment is not the type of worldview I propose. Nonetheless, there is an intimate relationship between appearances and the interior. They are interconnected, though the exterior is only revealed in its fullness through an encounter with the interior.

In a consumerist culture beauty is understood in an extremely narrow fashion. I am shocked when I look at photos of celebrity women—white, Latina, and black—and at times cannot tell one apart from the other. Part of the exploding cosmetic surgery industry is focused on the homogenization of the aesthetics of beauty. So one breast size, one type of nose, one overall "look" becomes celebrated as beautiful. If you do not fit into that very narrow standard of beauty, you are marginalized as ugly. This is equally true with hair type. I have what many Caribbean people would call *pelo malo* ("bad hair"). What does that mean? It means my hair is frizzy, curly, coarse, and unruly. I have spent half my life trying to tame my bad hair so that it looks like the beauty standard of straight, shiny hair. And I admit that I still do it. Why? Because I am not immune to the destructive and narrow understanding of beauty that consumerist culture celebrates.

However, beauty is never limited by the narrow ways in which humans understand the beautiful.

A Final Word on Shopping

Shopping is an everyday act. Emphasizing such an ordinary, everyday task in light of theological reflection is to give our everyday practices theological value. What is everyday life? Everyday life is the horizon through which we encounter the world. Daily life is not only material but cultural. It is something conscious, not merely repeated mechanically. It does not refer exclusively to the private or domestic sphere. Epistemologically, it is linked to what is known as "common sense." Daily life is thus the foundation of social systems. One cannot distinguish one from the other, for it is our everyday relationships that serve as the model for systemic social structures. Too often, daily life is seen as secondary to global, structural phenomena. Thus, while daily life continues to exist as part of reality, its liberationist potential has not been grasped. This in turn leads to a polarization of the public and the private, where life is not seen as an organic whole.

Daily life is the site of humanity's encounter with the divine and thus with God's salvific presence. Therefore, the lived faith and its daily expression is a central dimension of theological elaboration, its point of departure. In Latino/a theologies, for example, this emphasis on concrete life also appears in the centrality of popular religion within this theology. The everyday rituals that transcend the boundaries of public and private embody the holistic nature of daily life. Daily life ruptures the model of detached rational theology in order to take into account the fullness of human experience. It thus transforms the very nature and form of theological expression.

Though much of the shopping we do is for our homes and our own personal consumption, shopping cannot be reduced to the private realm. The feminist mantra "the personal is political" is one way of approaching this insight. In claiming that the personal is in fact politically significant, feminists are claiming that the personal has value and affects society. An emphasis on everyday life and its theological value becomes a way of politicizing the personal. The relationships we model in our homes are the foundation of our societal relationships. If you are raised in a household in which women are disrespected and have little authority, you are likely to be wary of women in authority in work and politics. To emphasize the value of everyday life is to highlight that our sources of knowledge need to be expanded from the private, abstract, and academic if we truly want to include marginalized voices.

We have discussed many aspects of shopping throughout this text. I began with an overview of the consumerist culture in the United States, where shopping has become an element of national identity. Shopping is definitive of who we are, who we value, and who values us. We constantly are bombarded with images that attempt to persuade us to buy the next technological innovation or the newest fashion trend. This consumer culture is based on the finitude of the goods that we buy. Goods are constantly replaced, things fall out of style, a new music player is released that makes the one you purchased one month ago seem clunky, limited, and obsolete. The culture of shopping in the United States needs to keep us wanting to shop more and more. Therefore, built into this system is the disposability of the goods that we buy. If we are not persuaded that what we own is not inadequate, we will not be pushed to keep shopping.

In addition to very concrete implications on people's individual lives, such as debt and living beyond one's economic means, consumerist culture in the United States values individuals by their capital worth. In other words, if you can't shop, you don't matter. The more you shop, the more valuable you become within the consumerist economy. This leads to three very destructive trends. First of all, one internalizes this understanding of the human and begins to judge one's self-value based on their financial potential. Success is narrowly defined as economic success. You begin to interpret your self-worth based on your role in consumerist culture.

> Too many people spend money they haven't earned, to buy things they don't want, to impress people they don't like.
>
> *Will Rogers*

Second is that you begin to judge others based on their economic value. The individual who is unable to shop, who is poor, is seen as lesser than someone who is able to shop regularly. In a capitalist economy if you do not spend, you do not matter.

A third trend is that through our rampant consumerism in the United States, we promote destructive practices toward the global (and national) poor and the environment. In our desire for more cheap goods to consume, we promote labor practices and working conditions that can be extremely dangerous for workers in the global South and in the United States. Here in this country we also consume at a rate that is destructive to the future viability of our planet. Yet we continue to shop even though our shopping is exploiting others and wounding the earth.

The second chapter of the book focused on Christian responses to shopping. This chapter demonstrated that the rampant consumerism characterizing American cultures goes against the core of Christian values. I do not take the extreme view that all shopping is evil and that Christianity is anti-materialist. I begin with an overview of Scripture passages that shed insight on the practice of shopping in the United States and our treatment of the poor. In citing particular gospel passages that challenge our obsession with consumer goods and the very act of consumption, I demonstrated that while shopping is not evil in and of itself, defining your life by shopping and defining others by their ability to shop is an impediment to leading a true Christian life.

My focus on passages that appear to vilify the rich and glorify the poor were not meant to evoke feelings of guilt and fear. Instead these passages serve to teach us that we need to reconfigure what we value and that shopping can come to impede our relationship with the sacred. It is not our wealth but what we do with our wealth that can become problematic. God, as I stated earlier, does not want anyone to be poor. But God does want us to live a life centered not on money and shopping but instead directed toward God. Foundational to this entire section is the connection made by Jesus between love of God and love of neighbor. An expression of our relationship with the sacred is our relationship with our neighbor. How we treat fellow human beings reflects our love of God. God is found in that neighbor, particularly the marginalized neighbor who may not look or speak like you but nevertheless is your fellow human being and child of God.

Following this biblical foundation, I turned to Catholic social teachings as one denominational resource for reflection on shopping. My intention in choosing CST was not to make this a "Catholic" book but to demonstrate how one Christian denomination has attempted to address the rampant culture of shopping that consumes the United States and is spreading throughout the globe. The foundation of CST is the common good. Contrary to the predominant individualism of the United States, CST claim that we are social in nature and therefore interdependent. We depend on each other and we depend on God. The principle of "the greater good for all," not just individual selfish advancement, should frame our lives.

Catholic social teachings also teach us that this common good (and here the teaching directly echoes some of the biblical passages cited previously) contains a positive obligation toward the other within it. We have a responsibility as Christians toward fellow human beings that we should see as a gift and expression of our love of God, not some duty imposed on us. Shopping is an ethical act. I concluded the chapter with some thoughts on how Christianity gives us insight into our relationship with all of God's creation in light of consumerism. Our understanding of ourselves and the implications of our shopping are cosmological, not just anthropological. I then concluded with a brief discussion of the prosperity gospel, a fast-growing movement within Christianity that legitimizes excess consumerism and materialism. I am critical of the materialism that this movement promotes, but it is, sadly, a perfect fit with the American culture of shopping.

My final chapter proposed a Christian reconfiguration of shopping. It is not a handbook on how to live your life or spend your money. It is, rather, a reflection on how we can embrace Christian values in our everyday practices, and yes, continue to shop. This is the most theological chapter in the book, because we must ground our Christian practices in the intellectual tradition of our faith.

I began by arguing that Christianity is not an anti-materialist religion. The material world is God's creation and is good. However, our distorted desire for material goods makes us embrace values and practices that conflict with Christian teachings. Basing my thought heavily on Augustine and his understanding of concupiscence, I highlighted the dangers of falling into a cycle of hedonistic consumption. This consumer culture can also lead to very destructive ways of understanding ourselves and how we treat fellow human beings. Shopping impacts the lives and livelihood of the global poor. Our consumer decisions should center on our solidarity with them, not the exploitation of them. The incarnation is the definitive moment in Christian history. God was incarnated in human flesh and creation was forever transformed. Our bodies have an ambiguous role in Christian thought and practice, and through my reflections on theological aesthetics I highlighted that the body is an expression of and not an impediment to Christian faith. The body cannot be reduced to a source of temptation. The material world is an expression of God's glory.

Underlying this book is the Christian belief that all of humanity is created in the image of God. The captivating passage found in Genesis 1 reveals that humanity is somehow distinct from the rest of creation, and that this distinctiveness somehow reflects the divine. I am often challenged to defend my interest in topics such as social justice, economics, globalization, and race, as if they have nothing to do with theology. Similarly, when I was a part of the mission in Guatemala, we constantly were attacked for our work in land rights, our fair trade coffee program, and our construction projects. Such matters, we were told, have nothing to do with Christian faith. The church should be worried about people's spirituality, not the price of coffee.

I disagree vehemently. The church, at least in this context, should be very concerned about the price of coffee. If you honestly believe that humanity is created in the image of God, then anything that degrades that image is an affront to God. As Christians, we must respond to these injustices. So much boils down to a misinterpretation of the image of God. We allow ourselves to stand mute as others treat our brothers and sisters like objects and not subjects, not recognizing their full humanity. In the dominant society's eyes, some folks reflect the image of God better than others. Such a bias insults God and negates the beauty of all of God's creation.

God's preferential option for the marginalized challenges us as Christians to embody that reality. It should not be easy to be a Christian. Jesus' subversive message got him killed by the dominant powers, and while Christians are not all called to a life of martyrdom, we are called to respond to the injustice that surrounds us. When I was an undergraduate at Georgetown, I was required to read the theologian Dietrich Bonhoeffer. Many things about his life and message made an impression on me; the one I will mention in closing is his notion of cheap grace. Bonhoeffer reminds us that Christian faith is costly; after all, it cost the life of God's Son. And what comes as costly to God cannot come cheap for us. We cannot cheapen the memory of Jesus by apathy; we cannot cheapen Jesus' message and the challenges it poses us today.

Proverbs reminds us that "the miser is in a hurry to get rich and does not know that loss is sure to come" (Proverbs 28:22). The miser here is so worried about acquiring wealth that he has no idea of the future that awaits him. Poverty will one day be upon him. This proverb should not be read as a prophecy of punishment. Instead it is a warning about the consequences of what we value. The man or woman who centers his or her life on material wealth and goods is not living a life oriented toward the sacred. This is a life focused on the fleeting material goods of this world, and in eternity this individual will most likely never want union with God, for he or she did not respond to the eternal promise of God's grace and love in this earthly life.

In Luke's Gospel, Jesus tells his disciples, "Sell your possessions, and give alms. Make purses for yourselves that do not wear out, an unfailing treasure in heaven, where no thief comes near and no moth destroys" (Luke 12:33). Does Jesus want us to sell all our material possessions and live a life of destitution? I don't think so. But we are challenged to reassess why we value the things we value and how those things become obstacles to leading a Christian life. The saying "born to shop" is not entirely untrue. We all have to shop. Shopping is part of our everyday lives. It is how we feed and clothe ourselves. Without shopping we could not eat. But a life ruled by shopping is ruled by something other than the gospel. If we "live to shop," then we are not living an authentic Christian life.

suggestions for further reading

The titles listed here serve as suggestions for further reading and also as a background to the ideas the author worked with in writing this book.

Alavarez, Julia. *Once Upon a* Quinceañera: *Coming of Age in the USA*. New York: Penguin, 2007.

Bales, Kevin. *Disposable People: New Slavery in the Global Economy*. Berkeley: University of California Press, 2004.

Beaudoin, Tom. *Consuming Faith: Integrating Who We Are with What We Buy*. Lanham: Sheed and Ward, 2003.

Crocker, David A. and Toby Linden, eds. *Ethics of Consumption: The Good Life, Justice, and Global Stewardship*. Lanham: Rowman and Littlefield, 1998.

Himes, Kenneth R. "Consumerism and Christian Ethics." *Theological Studies* 68 (2007): 132-53.

Hine, Thomas. *I Want That! How We Became Shoppers*. New York: HarperCollins, 2003.

Kavanaugh, John F. *Following Christ in a Consumer Society*. Maryknoll: Orbis, 1991.

McCarthy, David Matzko. *The Good Life: Genuine Christianity for the Middle Class*. Eugene: Wipf and Stock, 2004.

Miller, Vincent. *Consuming Religion: Christian Faith and Practice in a Consumer Culture*. New York: Continuum, 2003.

Pahl, Jon. *Shopping Malls and Other Sacred Spaces: Putting God in Place*. Grand Rapids: Brazos, 2003.

Schweiker, William and Charles Mathewes, eds. *Having: Property and Possession in Religious and Social Life*. Grand Rapids: Eerdmans, 2004.

Shell, Ellen Ruppel. *Cheap: The High Cost of Discount Culture*. New York: Penguin, 2009.

Underhill, Paco. *Why We Buy: The Science of Shopping*. New York: Simon and Schuster, 1999.

reader's guide

1. Would it be extremely difficult for you to go a week without spending money on anything that was not a necessity?

2. How would you define American consumerist culture?

3. Do you see excessive consumerism as undermining Christian values?

4. Are we in the United States entirely disconnected from the people who create the goods we produce? How could we become more connected?

5. The book discussed the quinceañera as an example of consumerism and religious rituals. Can you think of other examples?

6. What insights does Scripture offer us regarding the relationship between our spirituality and our relationship to the material world?

7. How does the New Testament challenge us to expand our notion of our neighbor?

8. What are concrete ways we can live a Christian life that crosses the chasm between rich and poor?

9. In what ways are our relationships with each other a reflection of our relationship with the sacred?

10. How do you concretely engage in solidarity work with marginalized communities? Why or why not do you engage in this work?

11. In what manner can Catholic social teachings inform our everyday shopping practices?

12. Do you interpret attention to the material world as somehow impeding one's relationship with the sacred?

13. Do you believe shopping is sinful? Are there types of shopping that are more sinful than others?